HENDRIX

HENDRIX

by Victor Sampson

PROTEUS BOOKS
London/New York

PROTEUS BOOKS
is an imprint of
The Proteus Publishing Group

United States
PROTEUS PUBLISHING
CO., INC.
9 West 57th Street,
Suite 4503
New York, NY 10019

distributed by:
CHERRY LANE BOOKS
CO., INC.
P.O. Box 430,
Port Chester, NY 10573

United Kingdom
PROTEUS BOOKS LIMITED
Bremar House,
Sale Place,
London W2 1PT

ISBN 0 86276 088 7 (p/b)
    0 86276 089 5 (h/b)
First published in U.S. 1984
First published in U.K. 1984

Editor Kay Rowley
Design Adrian Hodgkins

Discography by Chris
Charlesworth
Saville Theatre programme
loaned by Rob Mackie

Typeset SX Composing Ltd,
Rayleigh, Essex
Printed and Bound in Great
Britain by Blantyre Printing
& Binding, Glasgow

4

James Marshall Hendrix was born on November 27th, 1942 in Seattle, Washington. His father, Al Hendrix, was serving in the U.S. Army, and could not be furloughed for his first child's birth. He was not to see his son for the first three years of his life and in his absence, his wife, Lucille, named the baby Johnny Allen Hendrix. Lucille Hendrix, a beautiful young woman with high cheek bones and mocha skin, was part Cherokee Indian, but frequent bouts of tuberculosis often resulted in the boy being left in the care of friends or relatives for months at a time. When Al Hendrix returned from the South Pacific in 1945, his homecoming must have been a sad one. His marriage was on the rocks and his son was being looked after by a woman in Berkeley, California. Al went down and got him, brought him home to Seattle, and renamed him James Marshall Hendrix. Like many veterans, Al was hoping for a new start, but work was scarce after the war and he had no skills. He was living on a twenty-dollar-a-week discharge allowance from the Army and, for the next two years, lived with Lucille. Their reunion produced another son, Leon, before they finally divorced in 1950.

By this time, young Jimmy and his brother had been placed with Al's sister in Vancouver where they often visited their maternal grandmother, who was half Cherokee. Recalling his fragmented early years, Jimi said, "My mother and father used to fight a lot and I always had to be ready to go tippy-toeing off to Canada. My dad was level-headed and religious, but my mother used to like having a good time and dressing up. She used to drink a lot and didn't take care of herself. But she was a groovy mother."

Certainly young Jimmy revered his mother, and his grandmother too. They often told him Indian stories and legends late at night, but it was his father who provided the emotional continuity of his early life. In 1953, Al Hendrix brought his sons back to Seattle where a new job at last supplied some economic stability. Jimmy, now ten years old, was a quiet boy, shy and introspective. He must have been acutely aware of the pain of the separations that he had experienced and the seeming impossibility of emotional attachment, but he was too young and withdrawn to express his confusion and hurt. His silent, stoic manner was certainly a defense, a hedge against the inevitable time when he would again have to leave a home, but it left an indelible mark. Jimi, in 1969: "I was always very quiet. But I saw things. A fish wouldn't get into trouble if he kept his mouth shut."

Living with his father and brother in various Seattle low-income housing projects and rooming houses from 1953 through 1960, Jimmy was at last able to experience some of the more prosaic events of childhood, as well as some which must have deepened his growing conviction that this world was not a particularly hospitable place for him.

Although he joined the Boy Scouts and played end on the school football team, Jimmy never really enjoyed a peaceful adolescence. For one thing, Seattle in the 1950s was a predominantly white town, and Jimmy was aware that despite the early stirrings of the civil rights movement and the Supreme Court decision on integration in 1954, life was tougher if you were black and tougher still if you were poor. Jimi remembered feeling embarrassed about his clothes when he finally began to be interested in girls. Although his father was pretty steadily employed as a landscape gardener, the cost of raising two boys by himself was about all the family budget could handle and

(previous page)
photo: André Csillag

Jimi's unorthodox technique involved playing a right handed guitar left handed and upside down.

Leon Hendrix at his brother's wake.

Jim Marshall

10

Jimi's aunt who raised him.

Jim Marshall

Jim Marshall

there was little left over for luxuries. Further, Al Hendrix was plagued by various authorities who questioned the ability of a working father to raise two children and he often felt the brittle anger of one whose pride has been wounded by welfare workers, unemployment officials, or other well-meaning, but insensitive, civil servants.

By the time Jimmy was fourteen, his father had developed a taciturn, cynical edge, and communication between them was often restricted to stern commands from father to son. Jimmy sensed his father's bitterness and disappointment, but the general code of the household forbade any expression of emotion. No doubt he felt his father's love as well, but often it was buried beneath a fortress of reserve.

Al had a lot of records, mostly jazz and blues, and had been an adept tap dancer in his youth. There was always music in the Hendrix home, and by 1953, "race groups", like the Crows, the Diablos and the Penguins made records that were popular in the Seattle Negro community. In those days, the standard practice was for white groups to sanitize songs written by black rhythm and blues artists and to turn them into hits. Big Joe Turner's *Shake, Rattle and Roll* which was a million seller for Bill Haley and the Comets is a classic example of this "cover" process. But, in 1954, the rock 'n' roll juggernaut was approaching mass hysteria in the US and Jimmy Hendrix heard it everywhere. When Al Hendrix came home one night, he tripped over a broom in his son's room. He asked what it was doing there and Jimmy replied: "That's my guitar, Dad, I'm learning how to play it." Soon, Al gave Jimmy five dollars to buy an old acoustic. Al Hendrix remembers, ". . . It was just in him to do it. He felt it. It was no job, he enjoyed it. He just picked it up all of a sudden. He had no formal lessons. He used to practice a lot. . . . So many people tell me now, 'Oh, yeah, my son taught your son how to play. . .' It was just in him, and the guitar became another part of his anatomy."

It is difficult to credit that anyone taught Jimmy to play the guitar for the technique he adopted was quite unlike anything that a tutor might recommend. He was left-handed, but instead of playing a left-handed guitar with the strings reversed normally, he played a standard right-handed instrument and inverted the chord shapes that would normally be found in a guitar manual. This unorthodox, apparently difficult technique could only come naturally to a born musician with an ear for music: it could not be taught.

Jimmy's immersion in music helped him transcend the awkward early stages of adolescence. As he grew, his arms and hands seemed to belong to someone else, someone about six inches taller than he. Always lean, he must have seemed graceless and gangly, with his arms stretching almost to his knees. At about fourteen or fifteen, he started gigging around Seattle with high school bands. Jimi reflected on those first dates, "My first gig was at an armoury, a National Guard place, and we earned thirty-five cents apiece. In those days, I just like rock and roll I guess. We used to play stuff by people like the Coasters. You all had to do the same things before you could join a band — you even had to do the same steps."

Although he was still a raw novice (fellow Seattle musicians later recalled his playing as "mediocre"), Jimmy joined the Rocking Kings in 1958. The band played regularly around Seattle and Vancouver, performing songs like *Sleep Walk* and *Summertime Blues* (both favorites of Jimmy's), often receiving as much as ten dollars a man for a night's work. Jimmy also began to develop a stage presence as

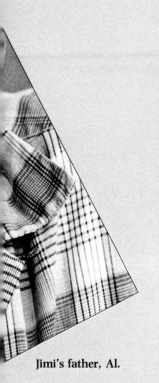

Jimi's father, Al.

he became more comfortable with his instrument, and the girls responded to him to the extent that his fellow band members resented it. A fight over his steady girl friend Betty plus boredom with the music led to his departure from the Rocking Kings.

Things were pretty much over for Jimmy in Seattle anyway. He had by now realised that he could do things with a guitar that dance bands would only scoff at, and his restless determination to get on with it was matched by a growing indifference to school. Despite Al Hendrix's urgings ("Man, you better finish. Finish this year."), Jimmy left Garfield High in his senior year, hung around Seattle for a while, and convinced his father to sign enlistment documents giving his age as eighteen (although he was still seventeen), thus enabling him to sign up with the US Army, 101st Airborne Division. Jimi, on how he came to join the paratroopers: "I figured I'd have to go sooner or later, so I volunteered to get it over with. Then I figured I might as well go all the way so I joined the Airborne. I hated the army right away."

Although the army was no more comfortable for Jimmy than the fractured world of his Seattle youth, Fort Campbell, Kentucky, helped crystallize his identity. Two more or less simultaneous impressions must have coalesced into a strange and disturbing concept that was later to find voice through his music. Firstly, as a member of the Screaming Eagle team, he made twenty-five parachute jumps (on his twenty-sixth jump, he suffered a back injury that led to his discharge). He claimed never to have had any fear ("It was more like a thrill."), but the sensation must have been exhilarating: suddenly released from the throbbing engine of the plane, floating between Earth and sky, hearing the fierce whistling rush of wind slice past him. The experience opened up a sonic reservoir in his mind and stimulated him to try and duplicate those sounds and emotions on his guitar.

Also in Kentucky he began to hear the rural blues of the South. In contrast to the unknown and ethereal sounds of the sky, the blues were rooted in the earth. The music came from decades of bedrock emotions, but so powerfully expressed the isolation and passion that Jimmy felt, that he was almost preternaturally drawn to them.

When his father sent him his electric guitar, Jimmy played constantly, even though he had no amp. He listened to Lightnin' Hopkins, Fred MacDowell, and John Lee Hooker and when he found out that Mississippi John Hurt and other bluesmen slept with their guitars, he adopted this custom himself.

The fragile camaraderie of men in uniform could not accept a man sleeping with and talking to his guitar and Jimi was consequently branded as a misfit. Inevitably, there were fights and other incidents and after fourteen months, the army was almost as glad to be rid of him and he was to get out. In his last days as a soldier, Jimmy fell in with a few other army musicians, including Billy Cox, who was also about to be discharged. Cox played bass, had some musical training and recognised immediately that Jimmy was onto something, although he too could not quite shake the notion that this Hendrix cat was crazy. Still, they got a group together and played around Fort Campbell as the Casuals. Their friendship deepened and when they were discharged, they headed for Nashville, playing in small-town bars along the way with pickup musicians.

By the time he left the army, the rough outline of Jimmy Hendrix was pretty much in place. He knew that he was a born musician, that he felt complete and at home only when he played his guitar. His musical influences, from the Forties jazz his father had played, to the dank, sexual R&B of the mid-Fifties to the Top 40 rock 'n' roll that had swept the country in the late Fifties and finally came to be dominated by Elvis, were shaped through the rolling delta blues and the aural blast of the sky. And by 1962, he realised that he was different from others. His childhood had passed without the support of home or family, he felt a repressed ambivalence toward his mother (when she died in 1958, his father had not permitted him to attend her funeral), he had never been comfortable in Seattle, and he had virtually been ostracised by the army. He was silent when other men spoke out and he heard sounds other men could not hear.

Perhaps, on a lonely bus ride through the Tennessee night, he felt the deep and unalterable sadness of the outcast and accepted, almost as a rite of passage, the fact that he would always be a transitory wanderer, a nomad. Perhaps this knowledge strengthened his resolve to find shelter on a higher plane, a safe harbour in the world of the spirit that could only be reached through his music. Perhaps he took some wry solace in the sureness that women could supply at least some passing comfort. When he played, they seemed irresistibly drawn to him, and when they discovered that the smouldering energy he generated on stage concealed a shy and gentle essence, they wanted both to touch him and take care of him.

So, as he pulled into Nashville at the beginning of a two-year stretch on the road, criss-crossing America by way of cheap hotels and smoky clubs, he felt a little like the blues singer Robert Johnson did at twenty – he might not have much else, but he was for sure going to have his music and some good times.

His music and the company of women were pretty much all Jimmy found in Nashville. He met Steve Cropper who, as the white lead guitarist of Booker T and the MGs, was an exotic phenomenon in the world of hip black soul music. The MGs were just about to have a smash with *Green OOnions*, Otis Redding had just released his first single, a country-soul hit called *These Arms Of Mine*, and Sam and Dave and Wilson Pickett were on the horizon. The time seemed right for Jimmy, but the demo Cropper cut with him – remembered as an undistinguished, if soulful, blues – went nowhere and by the time he left Nashville in late 1962, he was broke, starving and disillusioned.

He made it back to Seattle and picked up with a popular club band called Bobby Taylor and the Vancouvers. Through most of 1963, Jimmy played clubs in Seattle and Vancouver, until he signed on as a sideman with Little Richard.

Two years on the ''Chitlin Circuit'' provided an accelerated apprenticeship for a young man in a hurry. Little Richard's tour, the first of his many comebacks, was a rude awakening. Although Richard Penniman was a legendary figure of Fifties rock 'n' roll, by 1963 his brand of gospel-tinged Southern finger-poppin' proto-funk had been superseded in the national taste by the slicker, more heavily-produced black sounds coming out of Philadelphia and Detroit. Groups like the Tymes (*So Much In Love*) and a spate of girl groups, like the Chiffons (*He's So Fine*) and the Angels (*My Boyfriend's Back*), fought with surf music and classic white pop (*It's My Party* by Lesley Gore) for supremacy on the charts. The idiosyncratic fusion of itchy rockabilly rhythms and gospel testifying that pushed Little Richard to the top in the Fifties seemed dated by the time Jimmy got on the bus. But he was only twenty-one, and

Decca Records

endless one-nighters in deep south towns like Biloxi and Pensacola, formed an essential dues paying bedrock to his career.

Little Richard was an unpredictable and ungenerous employer. His constant need for the spotlight meant that the band played straight changes with little chance to stretch out musically. He was likely to fire somebody in some dead-end town in Arkansas if he got too uppity or flamboyant on stage. Even looking good was grounds for disapproval and Jimi remembered one night when his fancy shirt set Richard off: "I am Little Richard . . . I am the only one allowed to look pretty. Take off that shirt!"

Low pay, Little Richard's high-toned manner, and the narrow musical opportunities finally drove Jimmy out and he became an itinerant hired gun, playing coast-to-coast on package tours with R&B stars like Solomon Burke, Chuck Jackson, Ike and Tina Turner, and Jackie Wilson. A journeyman's life was wearisome; sometimes the music seemed mechanical, but there were occasional compensations. Every so often he'd get a solo spot and could depart from the standard arrangement to work in some feedback or a taste of the space-flavored blues inspired by Fort Campbell. (Often, the star or band leader would

14

be annoyed at these transgressions, but he was never fired.) Also, it was pretty much the norm for these shows to include a hot band number, often an instrumental, to warm up the audience. Jimmy began developing a physical performance for these tunes, borrowing moves from other guitarists' acts like playing behind his head or picking with his teeth.

Perhaps the most significant by-product of two years on the road was the valuable opportunity to meet and play with musicians he respected and admired. Still evolving his personal style, he'd listen and absorb the teachings of bluesmen who were playing before he was born. From B.B. King he learned to create liquid, soaring runs; from Albert King (who played left-handed and upside down, like Jimi), he acquired a knowledge of unique chordings and highly-individualised note shadings; and Muddy Waters gave him a good-natured lecture on the blues.

In early 1964 Jimmy took his slender reputation as a solid, if eccentric, sideman and his embryonic, but determined, desire to make his own music to New York. The broad tapestry of popular music was undergoing a radical and irrevocable change at the hands of three disparate insurgent forces – the Beatles, dominating the charts with energetic restatements of pure rock 'n' roll à la Chuck Berry and Eddie Cochran; Motown Records, an uptown black soul label (home of the Supremes, whom Jimmy had backed) with a contemporary attitude and a revolutionary stance, since it marked the first time a black-owned business had prospered in the music industry; and Bob Dylan, spearheading a hip urban blues movement and writing songs that embodied the personal intensity of poetry.

Settled in the Hotel Theresa on 121st Street in Harlem, Jimmy was conscious that music was changing. In the spring of 1964, however, he could ill afford the luxury of contemplating the meaning of these changes. He was financially strapped as usual, and looking for a gig. Harlem in 1964 was a bastion of jazz, predominantly the sophisticated variety, typified by Jimmy Smith or Chico Hamilton. Guitarists were generally of the Wes Montgomery school – melodic, laidback, slick.

Jimmy's hard-earned credentials as a high-powered sideman could not help him crack the Harlem establishment. He had a series of unproductive and frustrating auditions in Harlem's high-style night spots, where his weird tunings, performance antics, and feedback solos were singularly ill-received by both club owners and other musicians. But word got around that he was different and when the Isley Brothers were looking for a guitarist, Jimmy was a natural choice.

The Isleys were a successful R&B band, touring constantly and playing good rooms on the strength of their hits Shout and Twist And Shout (which the Beatles later took to number one in the charts). They played their own instruments, augmented by sidemen, and put on a hot raunchy show, up-tempo and lively.

Jimmy fitted right in. The Isleys liked him and encouraged his penchant for flamboyant clothes and a stage persona, which by this time included splits, playing with his teeth and behind his head, and some routines with his tongue that really got audiences up and dancing. He accompanied the Isleys to Bermuda and Montreal and played on a series of singles released in 1964.

Unlike the stereotype of the hired band musician, Jimmy was a pleasure for the Isley Brothers. He was no trouble at all, didn't drink,

Three of the major influences
on Hendrix' playing style
(top left) Albert King who also
played left handed and
upside down (bottom left)
Muddy Waters and (centre)
B.B. King

Andrew Putler/David Redfern

David Redfern

16

and could be counted on to show up. Off-stage, he was diffident and quiet, almost innocuous. He didn't seem to be interested in anything but music and when he wasn't on the road, he continued trying to break into the Harlem clubs or he practised guitar by himself, in a rented room without an amp.

When he left the Isley Brothers in December 1964, he played for a while with Curtis Knight and the Squires. Basically an unknown band, they played a funkier, more blues-based repertoire than the Isleys, and Jimmy was often the featured instrumentalist. For a time, they were the favorite soul group of the New York discoteque scene and they often played The Cheetah, a fashionable midtown club. After seeing Jimmy perform, people in the music industry, like Ronnie Bennett of the Ronettes, began to express interest and this strengthened his resolve to put together his own group. Les Paul, who pioneered the solid-body electric guitar in the early Fifties and is still regarded as an immortal in pop music, almost "discovered" Jimmy in a club in New Jersey during this period: "I went in and stood in the doorway to listen. I was really impressed by what I heard. Yes, indeed, that dude was really working his guitar over. He was bending strings, playing funky as hell. I'd never seen anyone so radical. We had to rush on to New York . . . but decided we'd hurry back to the club and nail that guy. When we got back, the bartender told us he was gone, that his playing was too crazy for them — too wild and loud, so they hadn't been hired. No one knew his name or where he could be found." For months, Paul conducted an "FBI search of my own," scouring clubs in New Jersey and asking other musicians about him, then finally gave up. Years later, when he met Hendrix and told him the story, Jimi laughed and said, "You mean I was that close and didn't know it?"

In 1965, Jimmy recorded a number of songs with Curtis Knight and the Squires. (Later, at the height of his career, this material was exploitatively packaged and released, giving the impression that Jimi was the leader of the band and failing to inform the public that the recording was over three years old. This classic case of monumental rock 'n' roll avarice caused Jimi deep and profound professional pain and resulted in a series of law-suits and injunctions which persist to this day.)

Jimmy's next gig, in late 1965, was a brief tour with Joey Dee and the Starliters, still riding the crest of the Twist craze they had helped start. The tour was noteworthy in that they played to primarily white audiences, who responded with enthusiasm to Jimmy's showmanship and stage get-up (which by now included an earring).

Jimmy began forming ideas about his own group during 1965, while he was playing intermittently with King Curtis and the Kingpins. Curtis hit big in 1964 with *Soul Serenade* and his hard, muscular sax sound was much imitated. The band was loaded with stellar musicians like Chuck Rainey on bass, Bernard Purdie on drums and Cornell Dupree on guitar; they offered Jimmy his strongest challenge yet and together they created a driving powerhouse sound, incorporating jazz, blues and R&B. Here, Jimmy's musical talents were appreciated and accented. Dupree reflected: "Only occasionally, when the spirit moved him, did he do guitar tricks and use his teeth." Rainey felt that Hendrix was happy with the Kingpins: "He never had a bad thing to say about anything. He was just happy to be included, but he was an exceptional musician. He had perfect pitch and was ambidextrous."

The Animals — Chas Chandler, later to become Jimi's manager (centre) and Eric Burdon (second from right).

The King Curtis band heralded a new plateau for Jimmy and the culmination of his Harlem years. In little more than eighteen months, he had established himself as a rhythm and blues guitarist of the first order and the progressive, original music of King Curtis was the highest expression of the genre. He was ready to step out.

While continuing to gig as a sideman, he formed his own group — Jimmy James and the Blue Flames — in early 1966. On balance, it must have been an exhilarating, if precarious, move. In its favor was the restless dream to play his own music which he had felt, if not always articulated, since Fort Campbell; the technical virtuosity he had attained in three years on the road; a stage presence and personal image that was nothing if not original, and an engaging innocence that drew people to him. On the down side, he had never fronted before and it was all too possible that the public would respond to a little flash and freaky feedback solos from a sideman, but might find it too spacey from a leader. And Jimmy must have known that the Harlem music scene wasn't going to give his new venture a tumble.

The changing shape of the three powerful currents in the mainstream of rock that were emerging when Jimmy reached New York also played a subtle role in determining his future. The English explosion ignited by the Beatles took on a darker mood through the blues-influenced rock of the Rolling Stones and the Animals, who were weaned on the same delta music Jimmy loved. Black popular music, nurtured by the liberating mid-Sixties spirit of civil rights, had completely broken down the old race barriers and permeated the charts and airwaves, evidenced by the Supremes, the Temptations and Wilson Pickett reeling off hit after hit. Finally, Dylan's dramatic embrace of electric rock 'n' roll and an angry, rebellious generation of American youth transformed folk-rock into a vehicle for protest about everything from an ugly war in Vietnam to attitudes about clothes and hair.

Harlem was pretty much insulated from the incendiary cultural impact produced by the English sound and Dylan, but Jimmy picked up on the signals. He particularly felt a sympathetic kinship with Dylan: "When I first heard him, I thought, 'You must admire that guy for having that much nerve to sing so out of key!' But then I listened to the words. My own thing is in my head, too." Like Dylan, he was interested in flexing the boundaries of his formative musical influences to accommodate his own vision, and like Dylan, he was accustomed to being regarded as a freak, a weirdo, an outsider.

When he brought a Bob Dylan album home to the small Harlem flat he shared with Fayne Pridgon, she felt betrayed. Fayne was Jimmy's first major romantic involvement. They had met in the Palm Cafe on 125th Street around the time Jimmy was making the rounds of the uptown clubs, looking for work. Fayne was a fine-looking woman, street-wise and independent, who knew many musicians. She was rumored to have been involved with Sam Cooke and had a weakness for "skinny, rambling guys." Jimmy fitted the bill, though Fayne thought: ". . . he didn't cut much of a figure. He had processed hair and shiny black pants that showed where the knees bent — but he had something about him, a *warmth*, that none of the other fast-rapping dudes had."

Fayne guided Jimmy through Harlem, which otherwise might have eaten him alive. She took him to her mother's home for dinner, consoled him after his fruitless auditions, introduced him to musicians she knew, and absorbed the flak from countless friends who wondered why she was wasting her time with him. Like women he had attracted before, and many he would after, Fayne responded to two divergent aspects of Jimmy: his vulnerability ("He was soft and easy like, feminine-like. He wasn't harsh. I'm talking about his demeanor now, his manner. I saw him go through so many disappointments.") and his prodigious sexual energy ("Jimi was relentless in the sack. He was well-endowed . . . and he came to the bed with the same grace as a Mississippi pulpwood driver attacks a plate of collard greens and corn bread after ten hours in the hot sun. . . . It was hard-driving and steamy — like his music.").

It was a volatile relationship and Fayne was threatened by Jimmy's total involvement with his music. He still slept with his guitar and would go out on tour or out to jam and leave her alone, jealously demanding that she stay and wait for him. As Jimmy's musical orbit expanded and he began spending more time in Greenwich Village than on 125th Street, they drifted apart, especially since Fayne was never completely comfortable in Jimmy's new downtown world.

Greenwich Village had a magical allure in 1966. Always a haven for the artistic and the unconventional, the Village became a shrine after the Beat Generation of the Fifties ascended from its funky streets. Wave after wave of would-be painters, poets, and musicians arrived to draw from and, in turn, replenish its creative coffers. By the mid-Sixties, the Village was a garden of cultural experimentation: hippies began to appear and with them, new drugs, new politics, new music, and new ideas about sex, all of which took root and thrived in the downtown hothouse.

Jimmy Hendrix was more at home in the Village than anywhere else. His clothes, his offbeat manner, and his music were almost nonchalantly accepted in this small universe of diversity.

Although the post-bop free jazz, unleashed by Charlie Parker and then John Coltrane, held sway in a number of clubs, the heart of the

Village, zig-zagging from West Fourth Street down MacDougal and across Bleecker, was given over to folk-rock and blues. An incredible roster of talent could be found at the Gaslight, the Cafe au Go Go, the Bitter End, the Night Owl, and Gerde's Folk City. Dylan came from this scene and Tim Hardin, Phil Ochs, the Lovin' Spoonful, Richie Havens, Odetta, Peter, Paul and Mary, Judy Collins, and Jim McGuinn and David Crosby of the Byrds, all incubated in the same four blocks.

The Cafe Wha? was of decidedly lesser calibre than other Village clubs and this meant that whilst record company A&R men and uptown tastemakers were checking out Arlo Guthrie just across the street at the Cafe au Go Go, Jimmy James and the Blue Flames played for tourists and college kids at the Wha? But they were playing regularly and Jimmy gained confidence as a front man. Audiences liked them, although they were not quite sure what to make of it. A skinny black dude with an earring and scarves tied around his leg, playing Muddy Waters tunes, not note for note and reverentially, but prancing across the stage, dropping to his haunches and spitting out high-volume distorted guitar riffs that were neither R&B, nor blues, all the while flicking his long tongue at an astonished N.Y.U. sorority girl, was possibly more than the audiences were prepared for!

Jimmy was befriended by the Fugs, who were often booked at the Players Theater upstairs from the Cafe Wha?. The Fugs (Ken Weaver, Tuli Kupferberg, Ken Pine and Ed Sanders) elicited an audience response similar to Jimmy. Playing drug-inspired rock, which embraced poetry, anarchy and performance theater in equal parts, laced throughout with scatalogical and sexual images, the Fugs both excited and offended their listeners. Though there was little in common musically, Jimmy absorbed some of the unusual fringe energy the Fugs generated and Ed Sanders recalls that they spent some hazy nights together, jamming in lofts with people like Buzzy Linhart and Jim McGuinn. Sanders later commented that the Fugs "helped Jimi grow his hair long."

Jimmy would disappear from time to time, to gig with Curtis Knight or Lonnie Youngblood, but he became a fixture on the Village scene. During the first half of 1966, he didn't seem to have a home, staying with his girlfriend Carol. He was always broke, often hungry, and alarmingly thin. Fayne observed that he never seemed to dress adequately for the weather. Drugs were a commonplace ingredient of the Village music community although Jimmy at that time smoked only hashish. In August of 1966, his guitar was stolen and he had to borrow to buy a new Fender Stratocaster. He was at a low ebb.

Fed up with R&B jobs for eating money, tired of countless nights in the smoky, claustrophobic basement of the Cafe Wha?, and generally strung out from an unhealthy life that brought him no closer to his vision, Jimmy was desperate for anything that felt like a change. The changes that took place in the next thirty days were so thorough-going, that by September 21, 1966, nothing, not even his name, would ever be the same again.

It began innocently enough. In August, John Hammond, Jr. had returned from a successful European tour and was booked at the prestigious Gaslight Cafe. An authentic white bluesman, Hammond's records of his own songs and acoustic-based renditions of Howlin' Wolf and Muddy Waters material sold well, if not spectacularly, and he gained a reputation as a musicians' musician. After Hammond heard that an outrageous black dude was performing songs from one of his old albums, he dropped into the Wha? to check him out.

Hammond later told *Melody Maker*: "He was playing a Fender Stratocaster upside-down and left-handed — one of those things that just boggles your mind. I just could not believe it — playing with his teeth and doing all those really slick techniques that I had seen in Chicago on the south side on wild nights. But here was this guy doing it, and he was playing fantastic blues. And he was incredible-looking. I asked how I could help and he said: 'Get me a gig, get me outta here!'"

Hammond had been playing acoustically (although Robbie Robertson played some electric guitar on the *So Many Roads* album Jimmy had heard), but on the spot, decided to use Hendrix as his lead guitarist for an upcoming gig at the Cafe au Go Go. They rehearsed for about a week, with Hammond playing harmonica and Jimmy's second guitarist Randy Wolfe (later Randy California, and a founding member of Spirit) on slide guitar. The blend was right. Jimmy knew Hammond's repertoire and his rougher, rockier style would add edge and character to Hammond's act, as well as the electric sound favored in folk/blues since Dylan's conversion. For Jimmy, John Hammond's engagement at the au Go Go was a godsend. Beyond the fact that he was making more money in a few days than in a month at the Wha?, the au Go Go meant more exposure and recognition, plus the possibility that a record company or manager might take notice.

It was a certified Village event. Hammond's stature as a musician drew the cream of the musical crop down to Bleecker Street, including most of the Rolling Stones and the Animals. Jimmy would pretty much lay back, supporting Hammond, but phrasing and bending notes in his own way, occasionally taking a solo and roughing it up with feedback. On his solo number, Bo Diddley's *I'm A Man*, he would unleash his own stage act, using every trick and move he had perfected over the last four years. The celebrity-filled audiences, particularly the English rockers (who gave quarter to none in their admiration for the blues) were overwhelmed by this unprecedented synthesis of sight and sound.

In no time, the village grapevine picked up the buzz and the heaviest musicians turned out to see "the incredible guitar player with John Hammond." Michael Bloomfield, then with the Paul Butterfield Blues Band and regarded as the premier American guitar player, came and left a believer: "Hendrix knew who I was and that day, in front of my eyes, he burned me to death. I didn't even get my guitar out. H-bombs were going off, guided missiles were flying — I can't tell you the sounds he was getting out of his instrument. . . . He just got right up in my face with that axe, and I didn't even want to pick up a guitar for a year."

High praise, indeed, and Jimmy must have been gratified to finally receive some attention from his peers. But the praise was directed towards him as a sideman and he was still playing other people's songs. He needed an audience to listen to *his* music and now, or the moment might pass. He might very well have slid back into oblivion, at least temporarily, had it not been for the persistent interest of Linda Keith.

Linda Keith was Keith Richard's girlfriend, who had come over with the Stones for their American tour. While Richard was on the road, she was ensconced in a midtown hotel. She began showing up nightly at the Cafe Wha? to see Jimmy James and his group. Her interest in Jimmy may have been more than musical and no doubt

Jimmy appreciated this fly white chick coming round in a limo and laying gifts and good food on him. But Linda had something more in mind, and she badgered and pressured Chas Chandler to come to the Cafe Wha? and see this new act.

As bassist for the Animals during their string of chart-topping hit in the mid-Sixties, Chas Chandler was a comfortable fixture in the upper echelon of the English rock world. He also had an uncommon intelligence and self-awareness and he was anxious to abandon life as a touring musician to become a manager or producer. Linda Keith forced his hand.

Hendrix and Chandler met at the Cafe Wha? in early September 1966. Jimmy put on his usual show, including versions of *Like A Rolling Stone*, *Hey Joe* (by Tim Rose), some Muddy Waters blues tunes, and a few of his own compositions. His singing was fairly tentative, as he had only been doing it a couple of months and didn't think much of his talents as a singer. However, he played his Stratocaster with complete abandon coupled with consummate control, wringing from it layered sounds — a thick and rhythmic blues bottom, then the kind of volume-enhanced power rock that reminded Chandler of Pete Townshend of the Who. To say Chandler was impressed would

Mike Bloomfield saw Hendrix in New York and "was burned to death".

David Redfern

be a gross understatement: ". . . I hadn't any doubt in my mind. To me, he was fantastic. I thought there must be a catch somewhere. Why hadn't somebody else discovered him?"

Before the evening was over, Chandler had offered to take him back to England and manage him. "He didn't just say 'Yeah, man, I'll come over to England!' He was worried about the equipment we had . . . and what the musicians were like. One of the first things he asked me was if I knew Eric Clapton. I said, 'Sure, I know Eric very well.' He said, 'If you take me to England, will you take me to meet Eric?' I told him that if Eric heard him play, he'd be falling all over to meet Jimi, and that clinched it."

Jimmy had only to receive his passport, and when he did, a few weeks later, the two left almost immediately. It was barely six weeks since John Hammond Jr.'s largesse opened the door for Jimmy Hendrix. Through the portal was London and Jimi Hendrix.

The lightning swiftness with which Chandler and Hendrix found each other and co-mingled their fortunes was a measure of how opportunely each fitted the other's needs. For Hendrix, Chas Chandler represented escape from his played-out role of backup musician and his first real chance to realise his musical identity, forged through the Fort Campbell sky music days, the lure of the blues, his finely-honed R&B chordings and the lasting poetic effect imprinted by Dylan and other Village musicians. The exciting London scene was attractive and he anticipated, with some trepidation, playing with the great musicians he'd been hearing about.

For his part, Chandler could not have found a more perfect vehicle than Jimmy Hendrix. He knew he'd hit on a talent in the same league as Clapton, Townshend or Jimmy Page. And, Jimmy was American, black, left-handed, sexy, and put on a show that left audiences in shock, all of which suited his plan to sensationalize Hendrix in the English press. Further, Jimmy was interesting as a man — shy and agreeable, yet full of ideas, musical and spiritual, that were far-out, yet perfectly in synch with the English freak movement that was exploring mind-expanding drugs and Flower Power.

Chandler and his partner, Michael Jeffrey, had a simple deal with Hendrix — in exchange for 30 percent of his total earnings and 7 percent of his record royalties, they would make him a star. No problem.

Chas Chandler and the newly-christened Jimi Hendrix deplaned at Heathrow Airport on the morning of September 21, 1966. When they arrived in London, Chas took Jimi directly to Zoot Money's house for an informal jam. Zoot Money was a well-regarded English blues veteran and Chas expected this casual visit would serve two purposes — first, it would allay Jimi's fears about being able to play with English musicians, and second, the word would get out that he was onto something special.

In the next three weeks, Jimi soaked in the London scene with Chas and participated in auditions designed to find a bass player and drummer, since Chandler had decided that Jimi's group was to be a three-piece.

It was important to move quickly. For all his enthusiasm and conviction Chandler had three major problems facing him: money, immigration and impact. To handle Jimi's introduction would require a reasonable start-up budget to support him, to wine and dine the press and generally make a good showing. Although Chandler's partner, Michael Jeffrey, was primarily responsible for funding their fledgling operation, Chas wanted to finance Jimi through earned revenue as soon as possible. Also, the English immigration authorities at first denied Jimi a working visa, waiting to be shown that he was a unique performer who would not displace an English musician by his presence. And the longer it took to break him, the greater the risk that premature press exposure would dissipate the impact of the emergence of Jimi Hendrix.

Jimi was fond of saying that Noel Redding was chosen because of his hair. He sported an unkempt, bushy red Afro, which made for a bold, almost ironic counterpoint to Jimi's liberated coif. In fact, Noel was a guitarist who had never played bass. Showing up for what he thought was an audition for the new Animals, he was willing to switch over to bass in order to play with Hendrix, saying: "I didn't see anyone playing lead guitar with this bloke." His guitar grounding helped Noel and Jimi communicate about the role the bass was to play — fluid, dynamic, active; it was to challenge the guitar, to set up a complex and furious atmosphere from which Jimi's solos could soar.

Chas Chandler also recruited drummer Mitch Mitchell who had recently been fired from Georgie Fame's band. Mitch had paid his jazz dues and acquired a thunderous, intuitive personal style; he was known to play the whole kit, rather than settling comfortably on the snare and bass drum as was often the case with rock drummers.

Chas Chandler told Chris Welch (in his biography entitled *Hendrix*): "The first time all three of them got together, they played non-stop for four hours."

By October 12, 1966, the Jimi Hendrix Experience was ready to be launched. Chas told Welch how the name came about: "We wracked our brains trying to think of a name for the group and we didn't find the Experience until after we found Mitch and Noel. Jimi had a few doubts about the name, but I said that soon it would take on a different meaning."

On October 15, Jimi sat in with Brian Auger at Blaises, a London club, and impressed Johnny Halliday, the reigning French rock idol, who brought the Experience to Paris on October 18th. Opening for Halliday at Olympia, the Jimi Hendrix Experience played their limited repertoire (*Land Of A Thousand Dances, Respect, Midnight Hour,*

Jimi, Noel & Mitch captured by photographer Gered Mankowitz

The Experience — Jimi with Noel Redding (seated) and Mitch Mitchell

26

Dezo Hoffman/Rex Features

and other R&B covers) to an enthusiastic response from a 14,000-seat sell-out crowd.

On the heels of their European debut, Chandler arranged for the Experience to play a series of carefully selected showcases at the better London clubs. The Mod underground, made up of musicians (the Rolling Stones, particularly Brian Jones, were often in evidence), photographers, fashion designers and models, began to pick up on the Jimi Hendrix Experience at clubs like the Marquee, Blaises, the 7½, and the Upper Cut. One night in November, Kit Lambert, the Who's co-manager, saw Jimi at the Scotch of St. James and flipped. Chas Chandler: "Kit nearly knocked over all the tables in the Scotch and wanted Jimi to be on the new label he was launching – Track. We made a deal that we would release the first record on Polydor, then join Track, which was not starting up until March."

In November, the Experience hurriedly recorded their first single financed by Chandler and Jeffrey. Although pressured financially, they nonetheless determined to make a record that would capitalize on the combined momentum of the underground buzz and the excitement generated by the press, which was about evenly divided between raves and hostility, the latter characterized by a not-so-subtle racist edge. Dissatisfied with the first recording of *Hey Joe*, they engaged Eddie Kramer to re-record the song. Kramer, a young staff engineer at Olympic Studios, captured its ominous dark quality and created a sound for the Experience that allowed a full aural spectrum of instruments to emerge (including a stinging, phased, floating-in-echo guitar solo), without losing the threatening character of the half-chanted, half-sung vocals.

Chandler thought he had a commercial record on his hands, but Decca turned it down. "The A&R man said, 'I don't think he's got anything,'" Chandler recalls. Running scared, he brought it to Kit Lambert, who volunteered to take it round to the record shops himself. Shortly afterwards, Polydor Records bought *Hey Joe*, backed with *Stone Free*, as a one-shot single, releasing it on December 16, 1966.

In addition to recording their single, the Experience played a succession of dates in November and early December. Mounting a direct challenge to the hierarchy of English rock music, which was focused around guitarists like Townshend, Clapton, and the Yardbirds' Jeff Beck, they quickly established a solid word-of-mouth reputation. Together only two months, they played with a raw newness which, when combined with a tendency to employ deafening psychedelic volume, worked to their advantage. The Experience sounded like no one else and seemed always ready to experiment.

Jimi immersed himself in London. He began to move freely, if shyly, in the circuit of pop royalty. There were parties with Brian Jones and Paul McCartney, flirtations with an endless string of women (including Marianne Faithful, then Mick Jagger's companion), and star-studded audiences at every turn, with luminaries such as Brian Epstein, Stones manager Andrew Loog Oldham and Beatles PR Derek Taylor in attendance. He stayed at the same hotel as Chas Chandler where Cathy Etchingham also lived for a while and his life seemed to revolve around all-night jams and late-waking days. He still slept with his guitar and spent a few hours in bed every day just playing for himself. He never seemed to have any money.

Chas Chandler was broke, too, when *Hey Joe* was released.

Although *Melody Maker* had given the Jimi Hendrix Experience a rave review after their December 21st gig at Blaises, calling Jimi ". . . one of the big club names of 1967" there were no immediate prospects for work. There was some uncertainty as to whether the public would embrace the Experience with the same fervour as the hip cosmopolitan club crowd. After all, the establishment press had taken to calling Jimi "the wild man of pop" and a "Mau-Mau", and it was quite possible that a racial, retrograde colonial backlash could nip this venture in the bud.

Chas had no choice but to deal with the problem head on. He pawned five of his six guitars to sponsor a promotional party at the Bag o' Nails on January 11, 1967. He hoped to promote the record and attract some bookings that would satisfy two goals: produce revenue and present Jimi to audiences outside the tight little London underground. Chas told Chris Welch: "He played the Bag and Philip Hayward, who was running some clubs, asked for him for £25 as a support group to the New Animals. I think the gig was at Croydon. From then on, Jimi never looked back and got regular work. I went to every gig and we spent an hour discussing it afterwards. He was still working out the act that was to become famous. At Croydon on that first gig, I think the audience were shocked. Their reaction wasn't excitement — I think they were numb! They weren't sure what it was about. Next we got a gig at the Roundhouse in Chalk Farm. Jimi got his guitar nicked and I was flat broke, so I had to sell my last bass. Two days later, *Hey Joe* hit the chart [entering at no. 48]. The DJs hadn't been playing it on the radio, but the word had spread through the ballrooms and it started to sell. I think we had about thirty shillings left between us."

As *Hey Joe* bulletted up the charts in January 1967, the Experience played a mix of dates, ranging from London in-clubs, like the Speakeasy and the Marquee, which generated flash and press coverage, to out-of-town venues, like the Beachcomber in Nottingham. By the end of the month, they were booked in London's top rock theatre, the Saville, sharing the bill with the Who, in what was considered a battle of the bands. Although careful not to play up the competitive angle, since there was a healthy respect between them, both Hendrix and Townshend pulled out all the stops, showering the celebrity audience with virtuoso pyrotechnics.

January 1967 put the Jimi Hendrix Experience over the top. On February 4th *Hey Joe*, still rising, hit no. 4 on the English charts and the press couldn't get enough of Jimi, looking for controversy and sensation in his every word. Chandler and Hendrix stoked the flames, making Jimi a cultural anti-hero, whose life and music embodied all that old conservative England feared in its polarized, drugged, and rebellious youth. And Jimi revelled in the attention, cleverly alternating his press quotes from serious remarks about his music to deliberately outrageous or ironic flights of fancy. On January 21, 1967, *Melody Maker* called his music "a weaving, twitching kaleidoscope of tremor and vibration, discords and progressions that give Hendrix the kind of color few artists ever achieve." Asked what his music tried to express, Jimi said: "It's the way we feel. We're trying to create our own personal sound and our own being. Our music is improvisation — no number is the same twice." A week later (January 28), when asked about his ambitions, he replied: "I want to be Marilyn Monroe's understudy, and I do mean understudy. . . ." When a reporter tried to induce him to reveal his techniques for playing with his teeth, Jimi told him: "I understand some guy tried it in a club the other night and lost three teeth. They don't know my secret . . ." he whispered conspiratorially, ". . . clean living."

In February and March 1967, the Jimi Hendrix Experience continued to gig, mostly performing material that was to comprise the first album. Simultaneously, they were recording at Olympic, with Eddie Kramer engineering and Chas Chandler producing. Jimi was also hanging out a lot, frequently with Brian Jones, with whom he developed an interesting rapport. The Rolling Stones were at a monumental crest in early 1967 (*Let's Spend The Night Together* had just passed *Hey Joe* on its way to no. 1) and Brian Jones at that time, considered himself leader of the Stones. Rich, notorious for his drug consumption, and resplendent in brocades and lace, Jones was a perfect symbol of rock's decadent arrogance. In addition to their outré images and behavior, Hendrix and Jones shared a taste for more exotic music than was the norm for rockers. They often hung out at the Cool Elephant, an exclusive jazz club, and Brian turned Jimi on to Eastern music from India with its eerie drone and different notation. Jones was an early champion of Hendrix and their friendship did much to keep Jimi loose and relaxed in the first rush of stardom. Jimi also spent time with Cathy Etchingham in her flat in Brook Street. (Cathy was Jimi's steady girlfriend for almost two years until Autumn '68 although this was not noised abroad as it would have 'spoiled' his image as a womaniser.)

Phase two of the Jimi Hendrix Experience conquest of England began with the release of *Purple Haze* on March 18, 1967. Written in the dressing room at the Upper Cut club, the song was an immediate hit. If *Hey Joe* heralded Hendrix's persona as a sexual outlaw, *Purple Haze* pushed his danger quotient even higher, revealing him as a psychedelic celebrant and an acid poet although ironically Hendrix didn't take LSD until after Monterey.

Laid in a throbbing rhythm bed and punctuated by phased cymbal crashes and a sinuous guitar lead that sounds like a cerebral corkscrew, the song has the physical effect of a heavy acid trip. Not surprisingly, the London underground heads embraced it as an anthem.

On February 25th, Paul McCartney praised *Purple Haze* in *Melody Maker*: "It's breaking through all over. Hooray! You can't stop it. 'Fingers' Hendrix, an absolute ace on the guitar."

As *Purple Haze* became a monster hit and the press was in high dudgeon about Flower Power, Carnaby Street and this black apostle of freak-out, the Experience left London for a package tour of Britain with the Walker Brothers, Cat Stevens and Engelbert Humperdinck. A photo taken at the time illustrates an odd, disparate assortment of performers. On one end, in a satin tuxedo, with string tie and Las Vegas teeth, is Crooner Engelbert (who Jimi came to like and almost envy for the power of his voice). Next to him is one of the Walker Brothers, a cute longhair, with a wimpy collegiate grin; then Cat Stevens, affecting a bored arrogance and holding a pistol (a prop from his act) vaguely pointed in Jimi's direction. Finally there is Jimi cradling his guitar, in this company a delegate from space, with ruffled striped shirt, silk scarf, and an exploding halo of hair. He looks straight at the camera, a little smile forming, and seems about to say: "Yeah, well, I don't know what I'm doing here, but maybe it'll be groovy."

To say the least. Although the Walker Brothers, then major teen raves, were the titular headliners, all of the artists had their own

Man bites guitar . . . Jimi at the Blue Moon in Cheltenham.

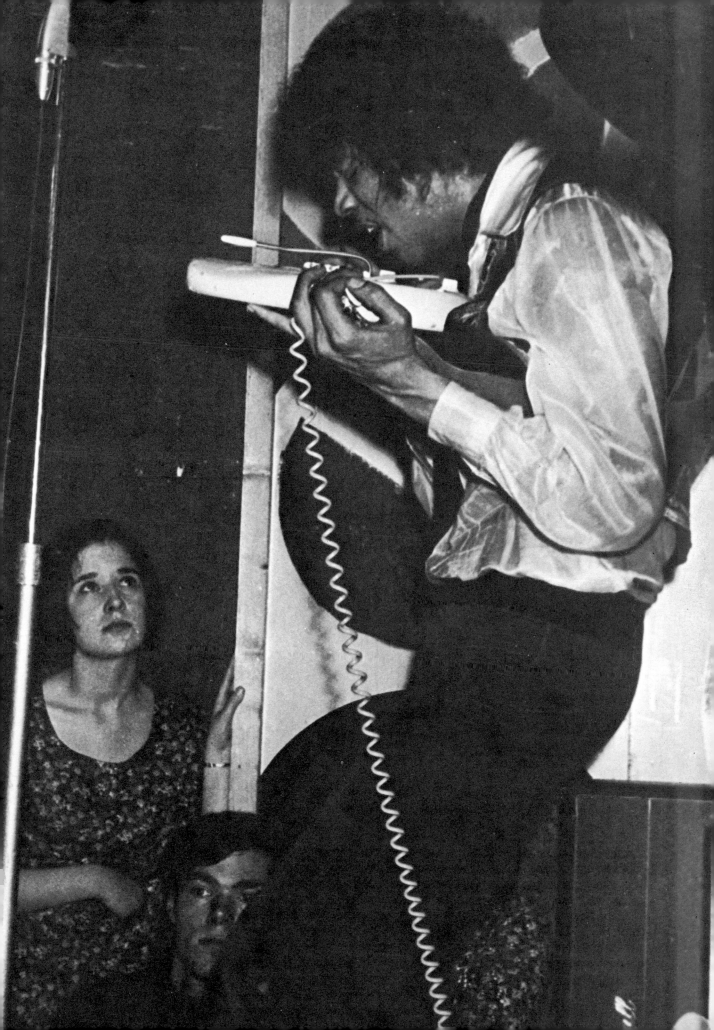

followings. The tour opened at the Astoria, at Finsbury Park, on March 31, 1967. Chas knew that the Walker Brothers ". . . were supposed to be the big sex idols of the time. But Jimi would cop all their reputation. So we worked on this big flamboyant sex act." Expanding and exaggerating elements of Jimi's stage presentation that had always been there, his show became overtly suggestive, an erotic invitation to the teenage girl fans of the Walker Brothers. To maximize the impact, management searched for something climactic — an apocalyptic touch that would shock and galvanize the audience. A few weeks before, Jimi had destroyed his guitar onstage in a fit of anger during a performance in Germany. Unexpectedly, the audience went crazy in an almost involuntary frenzy at the sight of artistic destruction before their eyes. But to smash his guitar again would seem contrived and rob the moment of its visceral energy. Chas: "We were sitting around in the dressing room, trying to think of something new to put in the act. I think it was Keith Altham's idea to set fire to the guitar. Jimi had been doing a number called *Fire* and Keith said, 'Wouldn't it be great if we could start one?'"

The end of the set. Jimi had gyrated and strutted throughout, humping and arching his guitar like a phallus, flicking his tongue at the crowd, drawing orgasmic crescendoes out of his Stratocaster as he writhed on the stage. At the climax Jimi fell to his knees, fumbled for a few seconds with a match, then leaped back as his guitar, soaked with lighter fluid, exploded into flames and screeching destructo feedback.

This was not just an act, this was an outrage. The promoters were horrified, the tour was met at every stop by committees of morally uptight citizens, decrying the "vulgar animal antics of Mr. Hendrix." The Walker Brothers, completely upstaged, were furious but powerless.

Needless to say, Jimi became a *cause célèbre* in the press, with sexual hysteria added to the list of his already flagrant excesses. To the suggestion of the *Sunday Mirror* that his act was obscene, he replied: "I play and move as I feel. It's no act. Perhaps it's sexy, but what music with a big beat isn't?"

By mid-May 1967, *Purple Haze* was no. 3, the Jimi Hendrix Experience was at full throttle, and all England waited in astonishment for its next move.

For all the furor he was inspiring, Jimi remained remarkably unchanged. Chas Chandler told Chris Welch about Jimi's personal response to the Walker Brothers tour: "Jimi had a ball, he loved it. It was then that it dawned on him he could be successful and do something big and lasting. It was then he got his confidence. If you didn't know him, it would seem he had no lack of confidence, but he was always very nervous and I had to talk to him before every show and tell him people really did like him."

Although he gained confidence, Jimi was still quiet and friendly and often embarrassed by attention. Paradoxically, his personal style was colorful and fantastic, and his clothing during this period was regarded as a symbol of extravagant social defiance. Dressed in purple velvet or 19th century military regalia, medallions festooning his bare chest, and pants indecently tight, Jimi was the perfect English fop, a dandy with an Afro. Asked about his wardrobe, Jimi laughed: "I always wanted to be a cowboy or a *hadji baba* or the Prisoner of Zenda."

Gerry Stickells, who joined the Experience as road manager in

A dandy with an afro

late 1966, formed a close, protective attachment with Jimi. He told Chris Welch: "He was an easy guy to get along with . . . He was easy to work with in those days because he wanted to get on. He was very keen and he seemed to know what he wanted . . . At rehearsals, Jimi said, 'We'll do this, this, and this,' and that was basically it. It was all pretty friendly, apart from Mitch, who could never be on time."

Jimi's instant success in England accentuated a strange duality in him. On the one hand, his stage persona was powerful and compelling in the extreme, and his lyrics and head raps indicated a funky cosmic intelligence that could operate with self-assurance and awareness. However, in person, he was so retiring as to be deferential, and he often voiced deep self-doubt. He particularly disparaged his vocal talents, telling *Melody Maker*: "I just wish I could sing really nice, but I know I can't sing. I just feel the words out. I just try, all right, to hit a pretty note, but it's hard. I'm more of an entertainer and a performer than a singer."

Somewhere within this dichotomy lay the insecurities of Jimmy the little boy, shunted from temporary home to home, and never sure of emotional acceptance. Perhaps only on stage, protected by the role of performer and distanced by lights and volume, could his true personality appear. At any rate, Chas Chandler, as close to him as anyone in 1966–67, confessed: "Jimi lived with me for two years and I would never presume to say I knew him. Nobody knew him. He never seemed to confide in anyone." Gerry Stickells makes a similar observation: "I don't think he had any close friends. To everybody, he had a different side. I don't think anybody knew him . . ."

On his return from tour, Jimi resumed the lifestyle he had been pursuing in London. He spent long nights jamming with Eric Clapton or Brian Jones and, on one occasion, Roland Kirk, proudly pointing out to the idiosyncratic sax genius that Handel had once occupied the house next door.

The first Experience album was being completed and Jimi grew fascinated by the studio process, watching and learning as Eddie Kramer experimented on the boundaries of recording technology. Hendrix was one of the first artists to understand and exercise technical control over his own recordings. The dense complexities of the Experience sound demanded that Kramer, Chas and Jimi invent new techniques in order to create on four tracks what would later be easily accomplished on eight or sixteen. At the time, attempting to duplicate the broad dynamics of the Experience's live sound involved such new configurations as recording backwards to create a flanged, distant sound, multiple layering of guitar tracks, achieved by bouncing from track to track, miking drums in stereo, and a host of echo, reverberation, and sound distortion devices, like fuzz boxes and wah-wahs. Meticulous care was taken to achieve each effect and sessions often lasted ten or twelve hours. As the album was readied for release and a third single, the lyrical *And The Wind Cries Mary* was put out, Chas made deals with Polydor in England and Reprise (distributed by Warner Brothers) in the US, the latter giving the Jimi Hendrix Experience a staggering advance of £50,000 (about $120,000) for rights to the album.

Are You Experienced? was a watershed album. It entered the English charts at no. 5 in early June 1967 and encapsulated the spirit of psychedelia then running at rip tide in England. Along with *Fresh Cream* (Cream) and *Surrealistic Pillow* (Jefferson Airplane), it became a

Next door neighbours – Handel and Hendrix

Kay Rowley

Karl Ferris/Pictorial Parade

legend on release. The English version (which did not contain the previous hit singles *Hey Joe, Purple Haze,* and *And The Wind Cries Mary*) marries the space imagery of *Third Stone From The Sun* with the simple, passionate blues of *Red House* and the hip, contemporary social attitudes of *Foxy Lady* (written for Cathy Etchingham) and the title track. In some ways the album's point of view is confused, a pastiche of sensibilities, but it is forcibly, savagely, held together by the relentless excellence of the musicianship and the tasteful consistency of the production. Jimi's playing, often double- and triple-tracked, is a primer in the art of rock guitar. He moves effortlessly from style to style, as convincing in his pounding metallic urgency on *Manic Depression* as he is in the deft blues phrasings on *Red House*. The title song, *Are You Experienced?*, offers the album's most telling statement. Flung out as an aggressive taunt, it forces the listener to take sides — on one side, the province of those who can "just get your mind together" is a whole new realm of sunrises and seascapes, the new kind of experience, accessible only to those who can leave their "measly little world"; on the other side, the old ways, locked in a sodden, unevolved unconsciousness. The song operates as a personal statement from a man to a woman, urging her to give up archaic, restrictive ideas and choose a new, free and sensual love. Finally, it is a statement of purpose, directly from the Jimi Hendrix Experience to the listener — release yourself to us, we'll take you on trips you've never even dreamed of. Jimi leaves no doubt where he stands, his final hissing answer — "Well, I have" — signifying a commitment to change, to evolution, even to chaos. As a coda, he makes it clear that you can get experience any way you like — "Not necessarily stoned, but beautiful."

Next stop, America. Although the Jimi Hendrix Experience stood astride the English music scene like a Colossus, they were, at most, an underground rumor in the US in June 1967. When John Phillips and Lou Adler (respectively, leader and producer of the Mamas and Papas) consulted Paul McCartney about "new" acts for the Monterey Festival they were planning, he vigorously proposed the Jimi Hendrix Experience. The Monterey Pop Festival was an event surrounded by positive vibrations. Conceived as a non-profit venture and supported by the spirit and energy of the musicians and the tribe of freaks who composed the first, highest wave of hippiedom, it was an exultation, a celebration of the new freedom of the Aquarian Age. Other participants included Laura Nyro, Ravi Shankar, Simon and Garfunkel, the Buffalo Springfield, and the Mamas and Papas. Otis Redding, finally crossing over to acceptance by a white audience, gave a significant performance. After years of dues-paying, he could not resist the temptation to chide the audience: "So this is the love crowd, huh? I'll show you some love . . ." Stunned by the roar of approval that followed, he delivered a stirring, heartfelt version of *I've Been Loving You Too Long* so charged with emotion that it brought him to tears.

On the night of June 16, 1967, in the wake of a show by the Who that left the stage smoking and the audience completely blitzed, Brian Jones, who had flown over especially for this moment, took the mike and presented the Jimi Hendrix Experience to an unwary America.

The Monterey audience was primed. They had seen Brian strolling with Jimi, who was dressed in ornate velvet and gold, hair bandanna-ed, sporting a button proclaiming "I'm a Virgin" and they heard rehearsals that boded well. They were also highly psychedelicized, courtesy of Owsley, the Acid King, who had been dispensing free tabs.

It is likely that Jimi had partaken of Owsley's generosity as well, and he was nervous as the Experience began their brief set, which included *Hey Joe, Like A Rolling Stone, Rock Me Baby, Can You See Me?*, and *Wild Thing*. As usual, the audience seemed mute with astonishment at the beginning, responding to the early numbers with respectable, though not overwhelming enthusiasm. Between songs, Jimi delivered a slurred, hip patter, introducing Mitch Mitchell as "Bob Dylan's grandmother" and blowing kisses to the crowd.

The audience responded warmly to *Like A Rolling Stone*, not only for sentimental reasons, but also because Jimi revitalized the song; he infused it with a street sense heavier than Dylan and, at several points, affected a kind of tough laugh, putting a sardonic edge on the lyric, and firing it home with dazzling frills and fuzzed feedback solos.

By the time the Jimi Hendrix Experience reached their finale, *Wild Thing*, the initial shock was dispelled and they held the audience in total thrall. Jimi introduced the song as "the combined English and American anthem" and the band turned the Troggs' hit of the previous summer into a theme of sonic and sexual release. Opening with a controlled feedback sustain that develops into a looping siren warning, underscored by Noel Redding's deep bass rumble, the song is held in check (Jimi works in a teasing phrase from *Strangers In The Night*) and focused on Jimi's insinuating vocal ("Aw, shucks, I love you") until Mitch Mitchell's machine-gun drumming signals a descent into a total freak-out that impels the audience to its feet. Jimi, who had used his guitar as a phallic instrument of seduction, biting and

Jim Marshall

Brian Jones and Jimi wearing his I'm A Virgin badge at Monterey

(right) During rehearsals at Monterey. Al Kooper looks on.

(previous page) Monterey 1967 photo: Jim Marshall

39

grinding, treating it roughly and then gently tapping the neck at maximum volume to elicit groaning feedback, finally dropped to his knees and set light to the instrument on the ground between his legs. Mitch and Noel improvised at peak intensity as flames devoured Jimi's axe, which fired out screeching treble cries and finally died in a high-pitched sustain. The response was bedlam, the audience cheering for several minutes, and the backstage scene was only slightly less tumultuous, with the notable exception of Michael Jeffrey, making a rare appearance at a live show. Chas Chandler told Chris Welch: "It took me 25 minutes to get through the crowd backstage. When I got there, all Mike Jeffrey was doing was tearing the group off a strip because they had broken a $150 mike stand."

Management tensions notwithstanding, the American debut of the Jimi Hendrix Experience had achieved its purpose. Through a combination of technical virtuosity and bold performance theatre, they had risen from obscurity to notoriety in one night. As Pete Johnson, in the liner notes to *Otis Redding/The Jimi Hendrix Experience At Monterey Pop* wrote: "Their appearance at the festival was magical: The way they looked, the way they performed, and the way they sounded were light years away from anything anyone had seen before. The Jimi Hendrix Experience owned the future and the audience knew it in a second."

In the first hot flash of their Monterey triumph, the Jimi Hendrix Experience was swept off to Los Angeles, where they were feted by the rock underground and there were star-studded jams with Stephen Stills, David Crosby, Mike Bloomfield and Buddy Miles (with whom Jimi renewed a friendship from his early NY days). KRLA, L.A.'s hip radio station, played *Purple Haze* constantly and there were hot nights at the Whiskey A Go Go on Sunset or at Peter Tork's house in Laurel Canyon, which Jimi described as ". . . . about a thousand rooms, a couple of baths, two balconies which overlook the world and Piccadilly Circus."

Management, meanwhile, was responding to the multitude of offers that flooded in after Monterey. In a move that further strained relations, Mike Jeffrey arranged for the Experience to open for the Monkees on an impending American tour. Although the Monkees were putting out hit after hit, their sound was manufactured and their appeal was to 13- and 14-year-old girls, not exactly the right target audience for the Experience. Chas Chandler: "Mike Jeffrey was jumping up and down, saying he had pulled off a great deal. We all sat looking at each other. I said it would be a fucking disaster and I wouldn't go. But Mike had signed the deal and it was too late."

Just prior to the Monkees tour, the Experience played a few dates in New York. They shared the bill with the Young Rascals in Central Park, and Chas hosted a press reception at the Cafe Au Go Go, where, less than a year before, Jimi had thankfully accompanied John Hammond, Jr. They helped Steve Paul's The Scene Club with an appearance on July 3rd, which was reviewed by *Variety* in their inimitable hyperbolic manner: "The Jimi Hendrix Experience proved to be up-to-date — i.e., loud — rock combo *sans* significant lyrics or vocal style, but avec the excitement of rock 'n' roll circa Presley. The trio pounds incessantly in tune with a contemporary format and Hendrix attains far-reaching electronic tangents on his guitar. Supporting him are Noel Redding on bass and Mitch Mitchell on drums, a duo of Britishers, who are well-schooled in achieving spike driving sounds and appealing presentation. Enhancing the physical presentation is Hendrix' colorful bejewelled attire, which combines the aura of Jerry Lee Lewis with that of Liberace. [!] However, for all the external personality, the root of the combo's appeal is its actual simplicity."

The reviewer qualifies his approval with what had become the standard criticism: "His sexual gestures are vulgar and will embarrass youngsters . . . in addition, his display of physical destruction to his guitar and speaker comes off as low class . . ."

In New York, the Experience sparked the same positive reaction among the cognoscenti that they had in Los Angeles and the media soon adopted Jimi as a new symbol of underground music. But the Monkees tour was, as Chas Chandler had predicted, "a fucking disaster." Too extreme for the Monkees' teeny-bopper fans, the Experience simply misfired. Chas told Chris Welch: "I met Dick Clark, who was presenting the tour and said we had to think of something – Jimi couldn't play to a bunch of twelve-year-olds . . . So, we put out a story about the Daughters of the American Revolution waging a campaign to get him banned. But as far as we knew, nobody from the Daughters had ever seen him. When I told Mike [Jeffrey] what I had done, all hell broke loose. He said I was a stupid idiot and shot off to Majorca for seven months. We never heard a word from the Daughters."

Mercifully escaping the potential fiasco of opening for the Monkees after only a few dismal engagements, the Experience got back on track. Chas had correctly reasoned that their constituency was the hip underground, then basking in the full bloom of the Summer of Love. Bill Graham invited them to play The Fillmore West (the epicenter of the Haight-Ashbury hippie eruption) on a bill with the Jefferson Airplane. After the first night, apparently recognizing that they could not compete with the sheer power of the Experience, the Airplane withdrew and the Experience finished the dates alone. Bill Graham gave each of the members $2000 as a bonus.

Jimi returned to England in late August to prepare for an extended European and English tour. Since Monterey, the Hendrix whirlwind had gathered velocity and they shot to pre-eminence in America as they had in Britain.

There were, however, some intimations of incipient strain. The Monkees incident, which disturbed Jimi (John Hammond, Jr. recalled that he was "bummed out about it"), had left deep scars in the relationship between Chas Chandler and Michael Jeffrey, although Chandler was still in control of the day-to-day management. There were seeds of discord within the Experience too. Noel and Jimi had a conflagration in New York, with Noel expressing anger over Jimi's telling him what to play. Also, the Experience rarely rehearsed, and Gerry Stickells told Chris Welch: "It was never as tight [after Monterey] and I think they got fed up with playing the same songs over and over again." Although they were realizing a healthy income, Noel and Mitch chafed over the extravagant attention paid to Jimi, and hints of a thinly-repressed racism could be detected (Noel had, on occasion, referred to Jimi as a "coon"). Finally, Jimi's personal excesses were becoming an inconvenience, if not yet a problem, to the Experience management. Not only was he freely experimenting with acid, but his dissatisfaction with the sound system and his tendency to blow up amplifiers, as much in anger as in theater, led to unexpected expenses.

To the outside world, the Jimi Hendrix Experience was riding high.

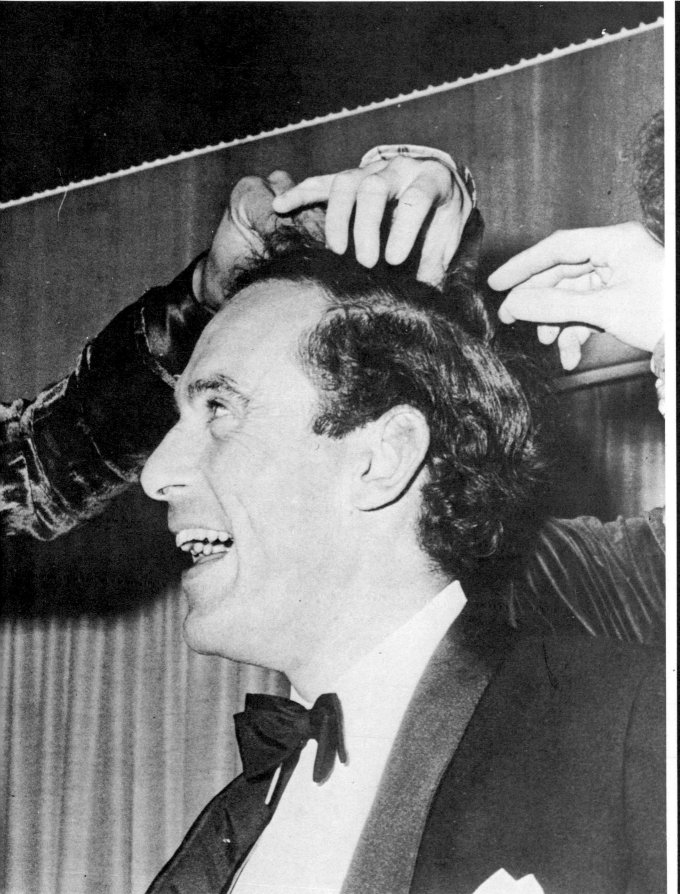

They were welcomed back to England as prodigal sons. Their new single, *Burning Of The Midnight Lamp*, had just entered the charts. *Are You Experienced?* had just been released in the US to critical acclaim and the new tour would preview material from *Axis: Bold as Love*, which was scheduled for release in November 1967. There were appearances on *Ready, Steady, Go* and *Top Of The Pops*, England's foremost TV rock shows.

For this tour, the Experience was to have a new sound system, supplied by Sun Amplifiers. In exchange for Jimi's "research" and input, the Experience would receive a full concert setup, which Jimi wanted to use in tandem with the Marshall Amps to which he had become accustomed. From the beginning, he had trouble with the Sun equipment, which could not deliver the power he was seeking, particularly in the mid-range and lower frequencies. On the early Scandinavian leg of the tour, performances often ended with broken amps littering the stage, blown either by choice or frustration. Despite the technical problems, the tour began in earnest with a performance at London's Saville Theatre on August 27th. Between sets, word came that Brian Epstein, a patriarch of British rock who owned the Saville and managed the Beatles, had died. In deference to Epstein, the second set was cancelled. After a series of European sell-outs, highlighted by a concert at the Paris Olympia, the Experience worked its way through the British Isles. Whenever possible, they would return to London to put the finishing touches to *Axis: Bold as Love* at Olympic Studios, with Chas again producing and Eddie Kramer engineering. They even recorded a theme song for the BBC's Radio One show, a jingle that had the same threatening posture as *Hey Joe*.

The pace was withering. Between the gigs, the studio work, the special appearances, Jimi began to tire. In November, he was filmed performing a blues solo, *Hear My Train A-Comin'*, his only recorded acoustic piece. Despite an elegant Spanish-flavored introduction, it does not hold up particularly well, offering palpable evidence that Jimi's most fulsome expression of the blues demanded an electric context.

A side trip in early December took the Jimi Hendrix Experience to Gothenberg, Sweden, where the pressure of the previous eighteen months was released in properly dramatic fashion on January 4, 1968. In a destructive fracas, more typical of the stage Jimi than the private Jimi, he wreaked havoc on his room at the Opalen Hotel. He had had a bust up with Noel and out of frustration (and too much alcohol), Jimi smashed up the room. The incident led to his arrest and he was photographed being led away to the local hoosegow in white fur coat and manacles. Released the next day, he was apologetic and paid sizeable fines, but the flare-up illustrated the fact that Hendrix had now risen to international rock star status, replete with drunken hotel-smashing scenes worthy of front-page reportage. Gothenberg also showed that the pressures attendant to stardom – long fatiguing tours, interviews and demands on his privacy, the need to give performances that surpassed their predecessors, and the omnipresent availability of booze or whatever – represented a hazard that the sensitive side of Jimi could not handle well.

Beyond the outcry of Gothenberg, Jimi was also expressing musical restlessness, although *Axis: Bold As Love* was selling like wildfire since its November release. Jimi told *Melody Maker* on December 23, 1967: "I'd like to take a six-month break and go to a school of music. I'm tired of trying to write stuff and finding I can't."

But there was no time for study or even thought of anything

45

other than a new American tour, a full-fledged extravaganza
featuring the Jimi Hendrix Experience, Eric Burdon and the Animals,
the Alan Price Set, Soft Machine and Nova Express. Arriving in New
York on January 31, 1968 on a chartered flight with the other
groups and a host of entourage members, the Experience was escorted
to the Copter Lounge atop the Pan Am Building in midtown New
York for a press party that had already been in progress for an hour.
Amid the pandemonium of reporters, TV cameras, rock scene *hoi polloi*
and drunken hangers-on, Jimi spoke to Jay Ruby of *Jazz And Pop
Magazine*. The interview reveals Hendrix in evolution and pensive.
Jimi responded to a question about "the destruct thing" by saying:
"There *are* times when we do it; but we play millions and millions of
gigs and when we do this destruction, maybe three or four times, it's
because we feel like it. It might have been because we had some
personal problems." After rejecting a comparison to Clapton ("That's
one thing I don't like"), Jimi and Ruby settled into a chat about music,
with Jimi illustrating his point of view using *Axis: Bold As Love* for
examples: "We try to make a change. You fix your life and say,
'We're gonna do this next time.' Then we get ideas — groovy ideas,
you know — everything's a very natural progression. I don't know, I
might not be here tomorrow, so I'm doing what I'm doing now."

"You don't want to put a lot of junk on top of it [the record], like
violins for certain numbers, unless it calls for it. All those things are
our own mind . . . all those things are coming out of us . . . like on
the last track of *Axis: Bold As Love*, it's called 'phasing.' It makes it
sound like planes going through your membranes and chromosomes.
That's the sound we wanted. We wanted to make the music itself
warped."

After a discussion on Charles Mingus, Roland Kirk and Chuck
Berry, Jimi was asked to define the blues. His answer affirms his
restless musical taste, recalling Fort Campbell, his R&B woodshedding,
and the powerhouse psychedelia of the moment. He is still open,
eclectic, and receptive to any music that evokes feeling: "You can
have your own blues. It doesn't necessarily mean that folk blues is
the only type of blues in the world. I heard some Irish folk songs that
were so funky — the words were so together and the feel! We have
our own type of blues scene. We do this blues one called, *If Six Were
Nine*. That's what you call a great feeling of blues. We don't even try
to give it a name. Everybody has some kind of blues to offer, you
know."

At the close of the interview, Noel made a telling remark that
summed up the philosophy of the Jimi Hendrix Experience: "If you
can't sit outside your music — outside one particular scene, man —
you need something done to your head." Jimi nodded in assent.

The tour was an unalloyed triumph. During February and March
1968, they played Phoenix, Anaheim, Chicago, Miami, Dallas, L.A.,
New York, and a host of midwestern cities to overflowing crowds in
large rooms. Chas Chandler and Michael Jeffrey had elected to receive
a percentage of the gate, rather than flat performance fees, and were
ecstatic at the reception and the profits. Playing material from *Axis:
Bold As Love* gave the sets a sense of freshness and the band sounded
terrific. In Cleveland, the local paper ran a contest offering free tickets
for the "Best Definition of Jimi Hendrix."

On February 12th, Jimi returned in glory to Seattle to receive an
honorary degree from Garfield High and to play the Seattle Center
Arena. Surrounded by a phalanx of reporters, he saw Al Hendrix for

the first time in seven years. *Rolling Stone* reported: "His father was floored when he saw Jimi in purple velvet cape and rainbow shirt. Not only did the elder Hendrix not realize how big a star his son had become, but he remembered his son as a conservative dresser with a subdued, reserved personality."

If his performance at the Center Arena caused *Life Magazine* to describe him as a "brash buccaneer with a wah-wah," Jimi was hardly the picture of assurance at his old school. So nervous he forgot his honorary diploma, he stood on the podium and invited questions from the audience, who had probably been admonished by their parents not to even look at him. In response to the one question "How long have you been away from Seattle?" — Jimi responded off-handedly, "Oh, about five thousand years." But the degree of attention focused on him seemed to make him uncomfortable and probably rekindled the subliminal sense of despair that Seattle had always prompted in him.

Other high points of the tour included dates with old friends Mike Bloomfield and Buddy Miles and their new group, Electric Flag, at the Shrine Auditorium in L.A.; with John Hammond, Jr. at Stony Brook University; and, in a stroke of inspired booking by Bill Graham, a night at The Fillmore East with that other shaman of psychedelic funk, Sly And The Family Stone.

Naturally, the American press, which had largely ignored his post-Monterey activities, or noticed only the most lurid aspects of his life and times, attended Jimi's every move. As *Axis: Bold As Love* cracked the American Top 20 on February 24th, an insightful review in *Life Magazine* by Al Aronowitz captured the essence of the critical response to Jimi Hendrix. Aronowitz balances his admiration for Jimi's playing ("Maybe the most gifted guitar player in the pop world . . .") and his lyrics ("His lyrics can seem to teeter at the edge of mush, but he has turned out to be too good a street poet to let them fall . . . Hendrix travels on the street of poets, paved by the imagery of Bob Dylan. 'I want to see and hear everything,' he sings, and there are moments when he makes you believe he already has.") with a prescient criticism of Jimi's showmanship and his use of sound for its own sake. Referring to the flaming guitar of Monterey, Aronowitz writes, ". . . From the flamboyance of that kind of gimmickry, rise the only clouds on this gleaming new star's horizon. Guitarists ought to make their instruments burn with their own passion — not with lighter fluid."

At a moment when *The New York Times* was calling Jimi "the black Elvis," Aronowitz, without detracting from his genius, implores Hendrix to use his guitar to "tell wordless stories of the soul."

The tour rolled on inexorably — 47 cities in 54 days, the prototypical rock 'n' roll caravan. City after city, hotels, drugs, women, whiskey, backstage scenes, sunrises, audiences deranged with anticipation, reporters, junk food, limousines, airports — after a while the hypnotic repetition of the experience obliterates any sense of reality beyond the moment and the moments tend to melt into each other. On March 9, 1968, Jimi told *Rolling Stone*: "If people only knew what state of mind we're in, like we're half there or not; like I don't even remember the Fillmore last night. I felt completely out of my mind."

The *Rolling Stone* report is a kind of loose interview — the *pensées* of Jimi Hendrix, and there are touches of Jimi's notorious cosmic rap. "I just thought about the title [*Axis: Bold As Love*]. There might be a

50

meaning behind the whole thing. The axis of the earth turns around and changes the face of the world and completely different civilizations came about or another age comes about. In other words, it changes the face of the earth and it only takes about a quarter of a day. Well, the same with love: If a cat falls in love, it might change his complete scene: *Axis: Bold As Love* . . .1—2—3, Rock Around the Clock."

Viewed in the context of *Axis: Bold As Love*, this seemingly spontaneous comment reveals an emergent Hendrix cosmology: The corporeal world is transient and bound up in small concerns ("Now if six turned out to be nine, I don't mind.") Through the assertion of independence ("I'm the one who's got to die when it's time for me to die. So let me live my life the way I want to.") and a willingness to be touched and liberated by a creative spirit (like music, as in *Little Wing*, Jimi's song about Monterey in which the "she" is not a woman, but a muse: "When I'm sad she comes to me with a thousand smiles. She gives to me free, It's all right she says, it's all right, Take anything you want from me, anything.") access to a higher plane is opened. On this plane, resplendent with auras and dragonflies and rainbows and flying saucers, the force of love, both physical and spiritual, generates change and growth. This change, the axis, charged with the uncertainty of the next instant, nevertheless knows itself ("Just ask the axis, he knows everything"). Perilously close to the ancient Greek concept of a prime mover or an Indian spirit, the axis moves forward ineffably and, through love, makes every increment of time immediate and everlasting. 1—2—3.

The underpinnings of this not-fully-realized lyrical premise are the sensations created by Jimi's guitar work on *Axis: Bold As Love*. Swirling, spinning, whipping from one speaker to the other, alternately attacking or caressing, the multi-layered guitars (thickened with echo, or treated with fuzz and wah-wah) are a sonic vehicle, transporting the listener to Africa, Spain or Space. With Jimi's vocals mixed to greater presence there is a more personal, less angry tone than in *Are You Experienced?* although some of the primal authority is lost.

Given the evolutionary direction of *Axis: Bold As Love* and Jimi's involvement in the technical aspects of recording, is it not surprising that he was displeased by the release of the Jimi Hendrix/Curtis Knight *Get That Feeling* album, on Capitol in the US and on Decca's London label in Britain. The result of sessions done during 1965 when Jimi was backing Knight, the album's release in early '68 (with Jimi's photo on the cover) was a cynically calculated attempt to exploit Jimi's success. Jimi told *Rolling Stone*: "It was bits of tape they used from a jam session, tiny confetti bits of tapes . . . Capitol never told us that they were going to release that crap. That's the real drag about it. It shows exactly how some people in America are still not where it's at, regardless. You don't have no friend scenes, sometimes makes you wonder. That cat and I used to really be friends. Plus I was just at a jam session and here they just try to connive and cheat and use."

Warner Brothers/Reprise secured a court order which temporarily enjoined the album's release in Britain, but it was only the first salvo in a back-and-forth legal contretemps that was to plague and unsettle Jimi for the next two years.

At the conclusion of the American tour, in late March 1968, the Jimi Hendrix Experience was one of the major concert attractions in the world, receiving up to 100,000 dollars for an appearance. The band and crew settled in New York to begin work on the next album. By now the Hendrix operation was a costly one: the payroll included road manager Stickells, equipment manager Eric Barrett, engineer Eddie Kramer, technical wizard Roger Mayer, and assorted assistants and advisors. Jimi was booked into the Record Plant, then New York's most advanced and expensive studio. With his passion for studio experimentation and the relative luxury that the newly-developed eight-track recording tape machines afforded, the *Electric Ladyland* album soon became an over-budget project.

The Record Plant was an easy place to spend money. Studio C was a comfortable place to work, plush and intimate, with soft-colored lights and a staff that was schooled in catering to artists' whims, Jimi took to booking it on a twenty-four hour basis so that he could work whenever and for as long as he felt like it, often beginning long after midnight. Sometimes Jimi would work for six hours just to get a guitar sound right; sometimes he'd roll in at 3 a.m., fresh from jamming at The Scene and, with five musicians and an entourage of twelve in tow, order drugs for everyone and record until the next afternoon. Chas Chandler, ostensibly the producer, lost control of the record and his artist. After fruitless efforts to keep the project in line, Chas pulled out in disgust, and subsequently sold his management share to Michael Jeffrey for $300,000. Jeffrey did not take the active day-to-day interest in Jimi that Chandler had, and the sessions continued with little management involvement.

In many ways, April to October of 1968 was a fulfilling period for Jimi. New York allowed him to establish a personal tempo and schedule that accommodated his idiosyncratic habits. He would spent night after night at The Salvation, The Electric Circus, or The Scene, jamming with the likes of Jim Morrison, Eric Clapton, Jeff Beck, the Chambers Brothers, Larry Coryell, Rick Derringer, Steve Stills, or whoever happened to be around. He particularly favored The Scene, on West 46th Street.

The Scene was the ultimate New York rock club. Besides booking the heaviest established acts and most promising new groups, the Scene was also *the* place for hanging out, with an endless reservoir of the best musicians, the best women and the best dope. Steve Paul, who owned The Scene, recalls having to beg Jimi to stop playing at 5 a.m., fearful that the police would close him down. Sometimes Jimi would play lead but often he'd play bass or rhythm and set up a killer backdrop for another guitarist. He played with John Lee Hooker one night and, for a while, with Jimi and Hooker sharing lead, the set went nowhere; then Jimi switched to bass and created a bruising physical fusillade of rhythm that inspired Hooker to a memorable performance. Johnny Winter, then emerging as the finest American white blues guitarist of the era, remembered: "We jammed together at The Scene a good bit; he'd jam with anybody who stayed there long enough. What we would often do after the club closed was go over to a studio where he had recording time booked regularly [the Record Plant, two blocks away] and play around with things, maybe play for several hours and then some other day listen to the tapes to pick out the good parts for ideas to work into songs." *Voodoo Chile,*

(pages 56/7) **Backstage at Winterland with Buddy Miles**
Photo: Jim Marshall
(pages 58/9) Photos: Joel Elkins/fpg & Gouert de Roos/LFI

Kennedy Stadium, Bridgeport, Conn. August '68.

David Redfern

John Lee Hooker was one of Jimi's early influences who later jammed with him at The Scene

with Stevie Winwood (then of Traffic) and Jack Casady (Jefferson Airplane) grew out of a jam at The Scene. The *Rolling Stone* review of *Electric Ladyland* noted that *Voodoo Chile* "sounds as though it was recorded late at night in a small club . . ." At the end of the song, maintaining the loose atmosphere, a girl's voice is heard saying, incredulously, "The bar is closed?"

Although Jimi was on a creative high between The Scene and the studio, there was still time for earthly pleasures. During 1968 he had met Devon Wilson, an imposing woman, tall, voluptuous and intelligent who had a personal presence enabling her to move as freely as Jimi in what was essentially a white world. She also picked up the rhythm and flow of his recording process and acted as a kind of monitor, letting people in or keeping them out, as events decreed. She became an unofficial liaison between Jimi and the Jeffrey office, maintaining a degree of order in an otherwise disorderly situation. Devon could also find whatever drug a situation called for and her own acquaintance with drugs was a first-hand one having what was described as a "vicious" heroin habit.

Jimi often kept a suite at the Drake Hotel, where Larry Coryell recalls an evening spent listening to Wes Montgomery and Jeff Beck records and drinking champagne and later he rented an apartment on West 12th Street.

There is no doubt that this New York chapter was a happy and fertile one for Jimi. Under the cloak of night and the relative

Singer Bowl, NYC August '68.

anonymity that the city could offer even him, he opened up and grew — in the studio, as *Electric Ladyland* became a two-record set; in the clubs, as the company of other stellar players afforded him the opportunity to play without having to simulate intercourse with his instrument and in his personal life, as repeated exposure to people with interests beyond music stimulated his senses.

Notwithstanding these positive developments, there were ominous signs of deterioration at the core of Jimi's world. The estrangement and departure of Chas Chandler left a void. Chas had been Jimi's weathervane and confidante, offering advice and guidance, both musical and otherwise and he had, in large measure, taken the pressure of the outside world off him. Michael Jeffrey was not interested in serving that function during the making of *Electric Ladyland*.

Simultaneously, the schisms within the Experience had grown deeper. Noel and Mitch were uncomfortable in America and not interested in eternal socialising. The interminable recording sessions were largely a drag for them. Noel recounted to Chris Welch: "He was always trying to do it his way. There were times when I used to go to a club between sessions, pull a chick, come back, and he was still tuning his guitar. Oh, hours it took! We should have worked as a team, but it didn't work."

Without occasional supervisory restraint, Jimi tended to run wild. Aside from his relatively harmless studio indulgences, he exhibited some alarming penchants. An unscheduled trip to Los Angeles during the recording of *Electric Ladyland* was punctuated by some major drinking episodes. He and Buddy Miles drank and screwed their way through Hollywood, throwing money away, until Jimi totalled his car and beat up a young girl. As a result, a Hollywood observer recalled, "There were some really bad cats looking for him."

Even as *Electric Ladyland* was released on November 2, 1968, the Experience was breaking up. Noel and Mitch returned home to England for a holiday, as the album "Produced and Directed by Jimi Hendrix" and featuring "Friends and Passengers" (including Winwood, Casady, Buddy Miles and Traffic's Chris Wood) was ravenously devoured by fans who had waited a full year since *Axis: Bold As Love*. It quickly shot to no. 1.

Electric Ladyland is an astonishingly dense and rich recording. Initially a disappointment to those fans and critics expecting another *Purple Haze*, it later came to be praised as a ground-breaking album for its imaginative use of studio techniques and for the broad spectrum of styles, textures and colors Hendrix achieved. Although the Beatles, Stones, and Airplane had all put out concept albums, Hendrix eschewed this form. Instead, the album is a kind of summing-up; with it, Jimi completes the musical cycles he had embraced, and without denying them, prepares to move ahead. *Rolling Stone*'s review of November 9, 1968 says, "Instead [of a concept] there's a unity, an energy flow."

Different cuts on *Electric Ladyland* suggest the different stylistic formats Jimi had taken on. Some of the songs (*Crosstown Traffic*, Noel's *Little Miss Strange*, *Voodoo Chile (Slight Return)*, *House Burning Down*, *Long Hot Summer Night*) are very much in the Experience mold — basic, muscular, with a furious rhythm bedrock lying under Jimi's sinewy guitar leads (often multi-tracked) and his vocals, nearly spoken, as they deliver aggressive, sometimes misogynistic lyrics. Other songs, like *Come On*, an Earl King tune that Johnny Winter

(previous page)
Jimi and Joan Baez backstage
at The Scene, NYC during
a Biafra Benefit concert,
August '68.

Jim Marshall

Backstage at Winterland.

Winterland, 1968.

Jim Marshall

69

(left and facing page)
**Woolsey Hall, Yale Univ.,
New Haven, Ct. November
'68.**

photos: Joseph Sia

remembers suggesting to Jimi, and *Gypsy Eyes*, have the basic R&B
feel that characterized the chitlin days, although his playing on *Come
On* carries the lightning bolt impression of his individuality. Still other
songs, like *Rainy Day, Dream Away*, and *Voodoo Chile*, feature the
guest sidemen and have a structured jam feel, thickened by the
textures of Chris Wood's reeds and Stevie Winwood's organ. Finally,
there are a number of cuts that have a quality Jimi described as
"sound painting." These pieces (*1983 . . . (A Merman I Should Turn
To Be), Moon, Turn the Tides . . . gently gently away, . . . And the Gods
Made Love*) feature a panorama of sounds that induce the listener to
believe that he is on a brief journey to Olympian heights or aquatic
depths. In fact, it was intimated that part of *Electric Ladyland* was
recorded in a studio filled with water (Eddie Kramer: "Let that rumor
continue — I like it! Actually there is an element of truth in that
because at one point we did put a speaker in a big bucket of water
and recorded it. But I don't recall which cut.").

Dylan's *All Along The Watchtower* is the single song on *Electric
Ladyland* that defies categorization. It takes the mystery of the lyrics
and marries them to the most perfectly realized instance of the
Hendrix guitar trademark, an eloquent talking wah-wah. The result
elevates the song to myth, the medieval character of the words
resonate through the physical insistence of Jimi's instrument. It was

critically received as a masterpiece and was Hendrix's strongest bid for a hit single in the US.

Back in England for New Year's 1969, Jimi underplayed the break-up of the Experience when he told Chris Welch: "Noel and Mitch want to get their own thing going — producing and managing other artists. In the new year, we'll be breaking the group apart from selected dates. Oh, I'll be around, don't worry — doing this and that. But there are other scenes we want to get into." Indeed, the Jimi Hendrix Experience was already re-forming, Noel having used the temporary split to demand that his group, Fat Mattress, open for the Jimi Hendrix Experience on the mammoth tour Michael Jeffrey had put together for the States during the first half of 1969.

Amid the controversy over the English cover of *Electric Ladyland* it showed twenty-one naked girls, some holding Hendrix album sleeves, the Jimi Hendrix Experience prepared for the tour, playing the Royal

Outside the Toronto court where he was remanded until June 19 on a charge of illegal possession of narcotics, Jimi signs autographs for fans.

72

Albert Hall on February 24, 1969, their first gig in England since mid-1968. It was not altogether successful since they were under-rehearsed and Noel, who had always bristled at the way Jimi told him what to play, had begun to depart from the ensemble nature of the band. Chas Chandler said that they sounded as if they were all soloing at the same time. To the disappointment of the crowd, Jimi didn't destroy his guitar or amp. In January, he had told London's *Daily Mirror*: "I'm moving away from what I've done so far. I don't want to play the guitar with my teeth anymore or clown around but I did it because fans, having seen me do it once, expected me to do it always . . ."

The scene surrounding Hendrix when he returned to the US in March of '69 was pressure-laden. In a thinly-veiled reference to Michael Jeffrey, he said: "People see a fast buck and have you up there being a slave to the public. They keep you at it until you are exhausted and so is the public, and then they move off to other things – that's why groups break up – they just get worn out. Musicians want to pull away after a time – or they get lost in the whirlpool." But management problems were only one component of the escalating intensity.

Everybody seemed to want a piece of him and he had a hard time saying "no." Strangers would ask him for money, groupies would press themselves on him, and people he hardly knew ingratiated themselves into his already-large entourage. On numerous occasions, he would find that the drink he accepted out of courtesy was laced with acid.

Further, relations with the Experience had not really improved. The American tour began on April 11 in Raleigh, North Carolina, under inauspicious circumstances. The next month saw constant gigging, often for grosses as high as $110,000, through the South, the Midwest and the West Coast. If the money was enormous, it was matched by the turbulent energy level of the tour. Members of Cat Mother And The All-Night Newsboys (a Michael Jeffrey-managed, Jimi Hendrix-produced act), who opened for Fat Mattress and Jimi, remember the tour as chaotic, but sometimes charged with a majestic excitement when the music was right.

Crossing the border to Canada on May 3rd, a routine customs search turned up several envelopes of heroin in Jimi's personal luggage. He was busted on the spot and bailed out several hours later. Although he had been known to experiment freely, heroin was not among his standard drug selections. He maintained, and it was widely accepted, that he had been set up; and there was a body of opinion that held that Michael Jeffrey was responsible, in an attempt to force Jimi to become dependent on him for help. Regardless of how it came to be there, the authorities had a case and the penalty for a guilty verdict was seven years in jail. Under this cloud, the tour continued, culminating in June with huge outdoor performances at Devonshire Downs (outside of L.A., for a fee of $125,000) and the Denver Pop Festival on June 29th, which was the last-ever performance by the Experience.

Jimi went into seclusion after the tour. Despite the fatigue caused by ceaseless touring, the dangerous deterioration of his relationship with Michael Jeffrey and the nagging pressures of the Toronto drug bust, he was in remarkably good spirits. Ken Schaeffer, a New York publicist, recalls that Hendrix "was always up, very giggly, positive, even when maybe he shouldn't have been."

In large part, Jimi's positive disposition can be attributed to his sojourn in Boiceville (about fifteen miles west of Woodstock, New York) and the collection of musicians he gathered there to play the music he had been conceiving, his "sky church music." Claire Moeriece, hired by Jeffrey to run the household, remembers that "it was the summer of the festival and a lot of people were up there already — Santana was there, all of Albert Grossman's people [The Band, Janis Joplin, Paul Butterfield], Taj Mahal."

Although Jeffrey had tried to insist on re-uniting the Experience, Jimi was forming a loose nucleus of jamming musicians, including Billy Cox (his old Army bandmate) on bass, Jerry Velez on the congas, Larry Leeds on rhythm guitar, Juma Sultan on percussion and Mitch, making a slight return of his own, on traps. Everything was loose, more open than the Experience. Jimi began to experiment more with the percussion adding an African flavor and the shape of the music took on undertones of jazz, particularly when Miles Davis' organ player, Larry Young, sat in. Apart from Mitch, Jimi's new band, unofficially known as The Band of Gypsies, Suns, Moons, and Rainbows, was black and sounded it. Although Jimi had said, "I just want to do what I'm doing without getting involved in racial or political matters. I know I'm lucky I can do that. Lots of people can't . . .", Michael Jeffrey was disturbed by this new direction, especially when the press reported Jimi's favorable comments on the work of the Black Panthers. (Jimi had indeed spoken with members of the Black Panther movement but did not endorse their policy of aggression and violence. He had previously donated $5000 to the South Leadership Conference after Martin Luther King Jr's death.)

The summer wore on. Jimi divided his time between his Catskill retreat and New York City, spending long nights (at premium rates) in the Record Plant with Billy Cox and Buddy Miles.

In June of 1969 construction began on Electric Lady Studio in the huge space that had been, until recently, The Generation Club on West 8th Street in New York's Greenwich Village. John Storyk, the architect who designed Electric Lady, remembers: "It was originally to be a club, with a small studio in the back. Jimi had been to Cerebrum [a multi-media nightclub] which I had designed, and the idea was to create a club that combined the sensory ambiance of Cerebrum with the hip rock 'n' roll of The Scene." But Michael Jeffrey reasoned that owning a studio would pay off, even if only by eliminating Jimi's studio costs. With Eddie Kramer as chief engineer (by this time working with Led Zeppelin, as well as other major acts), Electric Lady could be a major profit source.

Storyk's plans called for one big studio like the English rooms Jimi had become used to, and a smaller one, so that even if Jimi was constantly recording, there would always be a studio available for booking. In addition to a strikingly original design, with curved walls, variable acoustics, and architectural details that would accentuate the outer-space quality recording studios have, Electric Lady was to be a state-of-the-art operation, with the latest in recording console innovations and one of the first sixteen-track recorders. During construction Jimi would come in from time to time, and just look around or listen as Storyk explained what it would be like. He contributed little touches, like wanting round windows in the studio doors, so that it looked "like a ship."

Jimi would often stay in the city in an office townhouse kept by Michael Jeffrey Management on 37th Street. He would come by the

J. BAEZ

A. GUTHRIE

SLY STONE

R. HAVENS

COUNTRY JOE

J. SEBASTIAN

SANTANA

studio construction site in the late afternoon, sometimes in his star get-up, but often in jeans and T-shirts, and appeared so inconspicuous that on one occasion, Storyk recalls, the construction foreman didn't recognize him and asked him to leave. In the evenings he'd jam at clubs, usually The Scene or Ungano's, until 2 or 3 a.m. then he'd work at the Record Plant until morning, usually surrounded by fifteen or twenty people.

After a few days or a week on this schedule, he'd shuttle back to Boiceville — sometimes by helicopter — and arrive to a houseful of guests for a few days of jamming and easy living.

The house in Boiceville was always filled with people. Although

A French promotional photo advertising the Woodstock movie with Graham Nash next to Hendrix wrongly credited as David Crosby.

J. HENDRIX

JOE COCKER

Joel Finler Collection

it was secluded — two or three miles off the road — girls would find their way in and just hang around, hoping Jimi would pick them. Claire: "People would just show up to bring him beads and tigers' teeth and scarves and magic potions. Just every kind of trash imaginable. They found him." Claire Moeriece remembered an underage girl from Texas, who called home and told her family where she was. When a posse of state troopers surrounded the house, Jimi looked out the window and said, "Tell 'em I'm not home." There were always drugs, usually mescalin, acid and grass, but Jimi was only an occasional user and then in moderation. For Jimi, the house was a relatively relaxed and creative atmosphere. Once he and Claire stopped in Woodstock: "We got colored pencils and pads and Magic Markers. We sat around the fire and Jimi called everybody to come in and draw. He wanted everybody there."

The spaced-out communal nature of the house (sometimes things got especially weird — Claire recalled that once, everything in the fridge was spiked with acid) found its cultural apotheosis on August 19, 1969. The largest commune in rock 'n' roll history convened for the Woodstock Festival on that date.

In recognition of his status, the promoters had selected Hendrix to close the festival. He had come to represent the soul of the counterculture, the absolute integration of one's life with one's music and the achievement of a lifestyle that incorporated, in a competely outspoken way, the key ingredients of the New Age. He was stone-free, he was beautiful, unabashedly sexual, psychedelic, beyond race, beyond politics, beyond nationality, he was conscious, metaphysical, romantic, peaceful, and poetic. He was, to the 500,000 who gathered at White Lake, an emissary carrying their message — first, to the rest of the world and then, to the world of tomorrow.

Jimi worked with Mitch, Billy Cox, Juma, Larry and Jerry twenty-four-hours a day for several days before the concert. Between the rehearsals, last-minute negotiations (Jimi was to receive $60,000 for his performance) and nervous adrenalin, the intensity level was at the max. Finally, after some almost comedic transportation hassles (scheduled to arrive by helicopter, Jimi and the band ended up travelling in Claire's Dodge Dart), they went on in the early morning hours of August 21st.

Peaking on the acid and the tribal energy of the crowd, they did *Red House* and *Purple Haze*, by now Hendrix standards. They premiered a new song, *Izabella*, written that summer at the house, and played some of the jams they had recently rehearsed. It was a strong, if not brilliant set and would have sufficed, but the finale, in the muddy dawn, was extraordinary — an epiphany, a seven-minute statement, brought to you by Jimi Hendrix on behalf of the Woodstock generation. Jimi's version of *The Star Spangled Banner* wordlessly carved a vision of the New America. By turns, it was angry, violent, anguished, and hopeful. Massive amplification forced the sound off nearby hills, the echoes swirling orchestrally over the crowd. Jimi's guitar bent, dismantled, and then constructed anew the physical images of the national anthem, while the silent chorus, half a million strong, heard every word. Woodstock's America was distorted by firefights in Southeast Asia, chaos in the streets, cities choking in smoke and despair, hostile generations at war, but within, drawing from the spirit of the people, are the redemptive forces of change and love and peace.

Everyone was mesmerized. Jimi had articulated their own

Joseph Sia

Joseph Sia

testimony, their own inner voices. Some months later, he told *Life
Magazine*: "I can explain everything better through music. You
hypnotize people to where they go right back to their natural state,
which is pure positive — like, childhood, when you've got natural
highs and when you get people at that weakest point, you can preach
into the subconscious what we want to say. That's why the name
Electric Church flashes in and out . . . A musician, if he's a messenger,
is like a child who hasn't been handled too many times by Man,
hasn't had too many fingerprints across his brain. That's why music
is so much heavier than anything you've ever felt."

Claire: "Jimi collapsed when he walked offstage — from exhaustion,
total exhaustion. He just dropped." Michael Jeffrey whisked him away
for a few days and then began to implement his plans to capitalize on
Woodstock. He still wanted to re-form the Experience and he had
booked Jimi for another huge outdoor concert in Boston Common in
September.

Jimi balked. He wanted to transform his image. Instead of
destroying his guitar at Woodstock, he had used it to communicate.
He told Canadian reporter Ritchie Yorke: "A couple of years ago, all I
wanted was to be heard. Let me in was the thing. Now, I'm trying to
figure out the wisest way to be heard." The image that had been
created as his vehicle — wildman/superstud/freak — had outlived its
usefulness. Michael Jeffrey, of course, did not see it that way. The

formula that had made Hendrix was worth maintaining. For one thing, change could jeopardize the tenuous balance that kept a star at the top with a salary to match. For another, there had not been a Hendrix album since November 1968 and Jeffrey knew that the Experience lineup could record an album, have it out quickly, and not alienate the fans. The funky aggregation at Woodstock, given to nine-minute jams, might be too advanced for the record buying public.

The conflict was not resolved. Small compromises were reached. Jimi would not play Boston and a cover story about nervous exhaustion was concocted. Mike Jeffrey persuaded Jimi to do *The Dick Cavett Show* instead of a benefit for the Young Lords, Puerto Rican activists. The Cavett show was a surprising success, a soft-spoken and charming Jimi rapping with that paragon of obsolete values, Robert Young (Jimi knew best).

Jimi also got to play a free concert in Harlem. In 1961, he had knocked on Harlem's doors and been turned away; in 1969, came back to try again. Claire: "Jimi wanted acceptance from the black public. And he was a freak to them, an acid freak. They didn't want to know about nobody who took no acid. Forget the loud music. Bring me back some blues." If Jimi's free concert in the streets of Harlem didn't put him over with the black audience who still saw him as a visitor, as a gesture, it was well received. Downtown, it had an altogether different effect. Michael Jeffrey's fears that Jimi was falling under the influence of the Black Power movement increased.

Jimi spent the last three months of 1969 in New York. The construction of Electric Lady was proceeding, albeit slowly since, in the process of building, they had broken through to the Minetta River, an underground stream. The flood that ensued caused a month's delay.

Two other problems were resolved during November and December. Warner Brothers and Michael Jeffrey, through their lawyers, reached a settlement with the rapacious Ed Chalpin, who had produced the Curtis Knight album. On the strength of a seemingly unconscionable contract (Jimi had signed for one dollar), Chalpin had secured an injunction that had kept royalties tied up for the last two years. Choosing not to fight the matter in court, Jimi's lawyers reached an expedient solution: the escrow on royalties would be removed and Chalpin would be entitled to a share of all Jimi's future royalties and an album, to be released through his production company, on Capitol Records. There was widespread suspicion that the lawyers and Michael Jeffrey had sold Jimi out.

At least there was a favorable resolution to the Toronto bust. On December 10th, a Canadian jury acquitted him and the wire services carried a photo of a smiling Jimi flanked by two beautiful women (one was his friend Jeanette Jacobs) flashing victory Vs. As part of his testimony, Jimi told the court that he had "outgrown dope."

The album to be given to Capitol as part of the Chalpin settlement, was to be the Band of Gypsies concert, recorded live on New Year's Eve, 1970 at the Fillmore East. The Band of Gypsies had rehearsed throughout the fall, with Billy Cox on bass, Buddy Miles on drums and Jimi. It was more of a classic power trio than the Jimi Hendrix Experience had been, with Cox's simple understated bass and Miles' immense, but basic, drumming replacing the flourish and harmonic complexity of Mitch and Noel. Jimi's role had changed as well. Noel's guitar-like bass and Jimi's guitar had always set up a fluid, weaving,

Fillmore East, NYC on New Year's Eve 1969 — with A Band Of Gypsies.

UPI

Jeanette Jacobs (right) with
Jimi after being acquitted on
his drugs charge.

rhythmic structure, from which Jimi's solos emerged liquidly. With
Band of Gypsies, he took a more traditional lead position, soloing at
length, in front of a supporting rhythm section. One immediate result
was a greater concentration on the music and less on Jimi's personal
stage presence. In December 1969, he had told *Melody Maker*: "The
main thing that used to bug me was that people wanted too many
visual things from me. When I didn't do it, people thought I was
being moody . . . I wanted the music to get across, so that people
could just sit back and just close their eyes and know exactly what
was going on without caring a damn what we were doing while we
were onstage."

However, the *Band Of Gypsies* was not particularly well received.
Aside from a pounding *Machine Gun*, which Jimi introduced by saying,
"The next song is dedicated to all the troops fighting in Harlem,
Chicago and, oh yes, Vietnam," the concert and the album were
considered self-indulgent. *New York Times* review dismissed the songs
as "mediocre," and suggested that Hendrix had to be seen to be
appreciated. Jimi himself was not pleased with the *Band Of Gypsies*.
He told British writer Keith Altham: "If it had been up to me, I never
would have put it out. From a musician's point of view, it was not a
good recording, and I was out of tune on a few things. Not enough
preparation went into it and it came out a bit 'grizzly' — we all felt a
bit shaky. The thing was, we owed the record company an album

82

and they were pushing us — so here it is."

Less than a month later, the Band of Gypsies ceased to exist, directly on the heels of a disastrous appearance at Madison Square Garden on January 28, 1970. The occasion was a high-profile benefit concert for the Vietnam Moratorium Committee and marked the first time Jimi had "officially" endorsed a cause. Unfortunately, Jimi's drink had been spiked with acid and he was unable to play. He dropped his guitar and walked offstage mid-song, telling the audience, "I'm sorry, we just can't get it together." Johnny Winter's observation was: "I think it got to the point where people messed up his head so bad that he didn't know whether what he was doing was right or wrong. I saw Jimi backstage at Madison Square Garden . . .When I saw him, it gave me chills. It was the most horrible thing I'd ever seen. He came in with his head down, sat on the couch alone, and put his head in his hands. He didn't say a word to anyone, and no one spoke to him. He didn't move until it was time for the show . . . He never should have gone on."

On February 4th, Jimi gave *Rolling Stone* an interview. He called Madison Square Garden "the end of a big, long fairy-tale" and ascribed the aborted performance to "head changes" and exhaustion.

The bombshell of the interview was the announcement that the Band of Gypsies was disbanded and the Experience re-formed. Michael Jeffrey had orchestrated the reunion. The interviewer (John Burks), aware of the acrimony that had led to the break-up, was dubious but Noel and Mitch were seated right next to Jimi, confirming the change. Burks suspected that the interview was an out-and-out manipulation, designed to promote the old/new/old Experience and divert attention from Jimi's recent problems. He pushed Jimi on several points, asking him about his reported sympathy for the Black Panthers. Jimi: "I naturally feel part of what they're doing in certain respects, but everybody has their own way of doing things. They get justified as they justify others, in their attempts to get personal freedom. That's all there is. But [I do not support] the aggression or the violence, or whatever you want to call it." Burks felt that Jimi was evading his questions.

At one point, Burks asked Jimi if he had, in fact, "outgrown" dope, as he told the jury in Montreal: "Long pause, deep look on Jimi's face. 'I don't know. I'm too . . .' He has said this seriously All of a sudden, he flashed his little boy grin. 'I'm too . . . *wrecked* right now . . .' This was Hendrix the comedian. This side of Jimi is the one people love . . ." If Burks felt that Jimi's charm and apparent candor masked an ulterior purpose — to put forth the picture of a healthy, untroubled Hendrix and a "recontinued" Experience — he was on the money. Two weeks after the interview, Jimi's press representative phoned him. Noel had accepted a tour with Jeff Beck; there would be no New Experience. Instead, Jimi, Mitch and Billy Cox would tour, beginning in April.

Photographer Ira Cohen shot the Experience on the same day as the *Rolling Stone* interview and reminisced: "There was this tension . . . there were problems between them. I wanted to try and get them very close . . . into a knot, almost . . . But they were rigid . . . So I thought the best thing might be to photograph them separately and then work them back in together. Then somebody said, 'Jimi's just leaving.' I ran after him and brought him back . . . He wasn't saying, 'Fuck you, man, I'm leaving . . .' He was just in some strange mood . . . All the times I met him, he was in some kind of mood."

isparate influences were affecting Jimi throughout early 1970. While recording at the Record Plant in mid-'69, he had met Alan Douglas. Douglas had produced The Last Poets and John McLaughlin's debut album and he encouraged Jimi to expand his horizons, introducing him to jazz musicians including McLaughlin and Tony Williams, who was then playing with Miles Davis. Jamming with these musicians and other high-calibre jazz players helped solidify Jimi's intent to return to a funkier R&B *cum* jazz funk style. In interviews, Jimi mentioned his desire to play with Miles Davis and Gil Evans, and during early 1970 some of the material for a new two-record set, tentatively titled *First Rays Of The New Rising Sun*, was recorded.

Douglas fulfilled another important function for Jimi. Despite the success Michael Jeffrey had achieved for him, their relationship had finally come apart. His management contract with Jeffrey was due to expire in October 1970 and it was common knowledge that Jimi did not intend to re-sign. Douglas, like Jeffrey, had plenty of style and professional assurance but was easier to relate to musically and socially. Where Jeffrey was somewhat of a crude rock 'n' roll entrepreneur, Douglas had class.

Ira Cohen, who photographed for Douglas Records, sketched the relationship: "They seemed to be in pretty warm and personal contact. Alan is a very charming guy. He'd turn you on, talk to you, like a man, like a brother. He was always interested in supporting and doing things, but of course, he was also looking for what would be commercially successful . . . Alan was an ultimate hipster."

There was a scene around Douglas that attracted Jimi, although Cohen remembers that he'd often hang around the office like a "sad and homeless urchin looking for a little attention." He was also looking for the guidance and understanding that the Jeffrey management organization no longer provided. (To the extent that Douglas and his staff took charge of him, they did Jeffrey a favor, often seeing to it that Jimi would show up when and where he was supposed to, instead of disappearing for a few days.)

Mike Jeffrey, Hendrix's manager.

Jim Marshall

Also, Jimi was spending time with Alan Douglas' wife Stella and her cousin Collette and was often to be found in their East Village boutique where they made his stage clothes, sometimes pretending to be a salesman for a laugh. Ira Cohen felt that they "had him by the nose in some way" and Claire Moeriece called Stella and Collette "death chicks," but Jimi was intrigued by their sophisticated blend of independence and hard-edged intelligence.

Michael Jeffrey became concerned that he was losing control over Jimi and when he discovered that Jimi had been spending so much time in the studio, he came down hard, threatening Douglas with lawsuits and other, less conventional, reprisals.

The spring tour of 1970 reflected the divisive nature of Jimi's career. He opened at the Forum in Los Angeles on April 25th, with a drummer in the old Hendrix image – Mitch Mitchell – and a bassist in the new – Billy Cox. They played familiar material from *Are You Experienced?* and long, unrecognized pieces from *Band Of Gypsies* (to be released in May) and the still-in-progress *First Rays Of The New Rising Sun*, like *Belly Button Window* and *Midnight Lightning*. The tenor of the Forum show was more subdued than previous Hendrix performances in L.A., particularly to audiences still screaming for psychedelia. At one point during the tour, when a fan yelled out for *Hey Joe*, Jimi snarled, "I ain't no juke box."

The Berkeley concert on May 30, 1970, which was filmed and released as *Jimi Plays Berkeley*, was closer to vintage Hendrix. The concert took place as Berkeley was erupting in pitched battles between police and protesters, angry over American incursions into Laos and Cambodia and atrocities committed at Kent State. The film contrasts Jimi's arrival in a limo at the Community Theatre (with Devon and Collette) and the seething, incipient riots in the streets.

Jimi Plays Berkeley demonstrates the degree to which Jimi's virtuosity had grown since Monterey. Where Monterey had been a full-frontal assault, with the impact of a locomotive, Berkeley is more a precision jet flight, with Jimi the pilot, in subtle control. He uses his white Stratocaster like an extension of his body, coaxing whines and shrieks as he forces it against the mike stand, gently tapping the neck and manipulating the whang bar like a lover, to make it moan and cry. The urgency is sustained and the mood reflects the political struggle outside the doors and the sexual excitement within the auditorium. *The Star-Spangled Banner* is stronger even than it was at Woodstock: at one point Jimi, who has just used his guitar to simulate bomb explosions, police sirens, and an F-1 piercing the Vietnam sky, speaks: "Big deal." The comment is laced with sarcasm towards the national behavior in Vietnam and on the Berkeley campus. Later, he rips off an inspired *Johnny B. Goode* at breakneck speed, playing rhythm and lead simultaneously in an almost flawless performance. When his sustained feedback gets away from him for an instant, he turns and looks at the offending amp in disbelief. The rest of the set is just as masterful, including a full-tilt rendition of *Purple Haze*, complete with teeth-playing and tongue flicking. On *Voodoo Chile*, the film's last song, the camera captures the interplay between Hendrix and two young girls, maybe fifteen, who have worked their way to the edge of the stage. Thrusting his guitar at them like a red-hot instrument of pleasure, Jimi drops to his knees, three feet from stage front, leans back and simulates cunnilingus with his instrument. The girls, their innocence threatened by their own imaginations, are forced to cover their eyes and giggle; it was just

Atlanta Pop Festival, 1970.

87

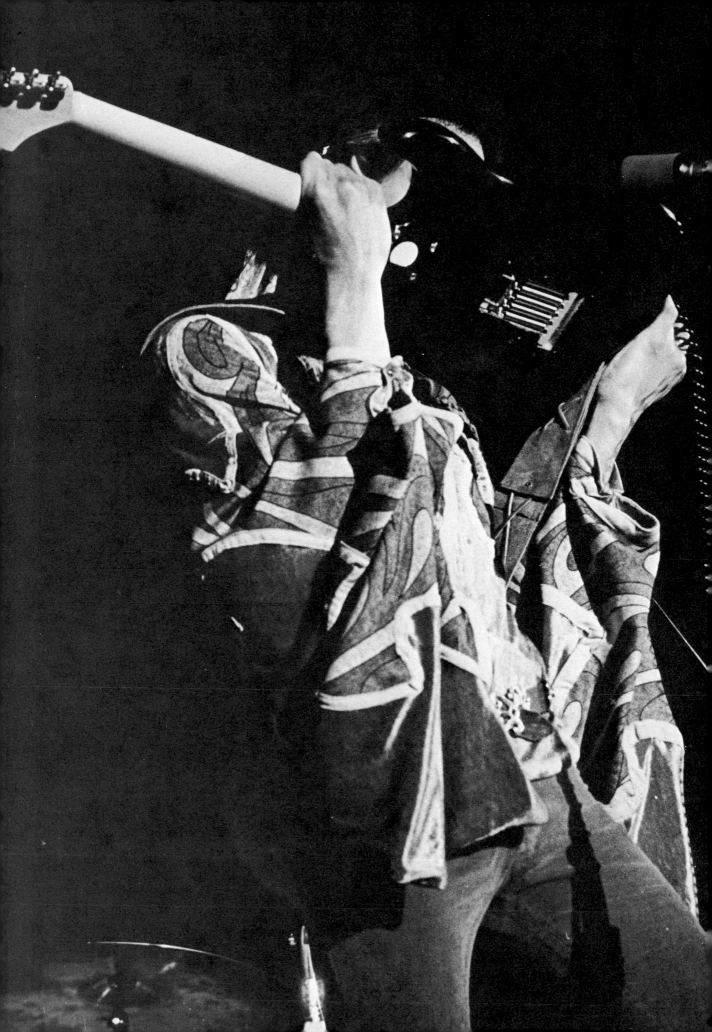

too much.

On July 4th, Jimi and band played the Atlanta Pop Festival. A few weeks later, they participated in the Rainbow Bridge concerts on Maui, Hawaii, which spawned a film entitled *Rainbow Bridge*. In keeping with the cosmic spirit of the event Jimi played a set that was instrumentally majestic but vocally sloppy. The sound was enhanced by the perfect natural acoustics of the volcanic crater that housed the concert.

During breaks in the performing schedule, Jimi would rush back to New York. His personal pace was accelerating as Electric Lady neared completion. In May and June he spent long hours there alone, recording with Eddie Kramer even before the studio could accommodate a full band set-up. John Storyk recalls several instances when workmen would arrive at eight or nine in the morning to find Jimi still recording. By July the studio was completed and Jimi moved in with a vengeance, as if he knew there wasn't much time left. The final cost of the project (which had been budgeted for $350,000) exceeded a million dollars. *The Village Voice* said it had "Alphaville class" and represented the pinnacle of recording studio design up to that point. And, at $1,000,000, it represented a huge gamble for Michael Jeffrey, since his star had had an inconsistent eighteen months. Only Woodstock stood out as a really stellar achievement since the *Electric Ladyland* album, and the commercial departure of *First Rays Of The New Rising Sun* was now on the horizon. But to Jimi, Electric Lady was the closest he ever had to a real home where he could come and go as he pleased.

After the Rainbow Bridge concert Jimi came off the road and settled into Electric Lady for an extended and prodigious burst of recording. He had his management postpone a scheduled return to England on August 13th and, with Eddie Kramer, sequestered himself in the studio to continue work on *First Rays Of The New Rising Sun*. There was clearly enough material for a double album, including many tracks recorded during 1969 at the Record Plant and new songs with Mitch, Billy and assorted guests like the Ronettes, the Ghetto Fighters (Arthur and Albert Allen, funky black vocalists Jimi had taken a liking to) and Juma Sultan. Alan Douglas had been temporarily stalemated by Michael Jeffrey but he, Jimi, Stella, Collette and Devon continued to socialise regularly.

If the completion of Electric Lady and the freedom to experiment at length in his new studio were creatively liberating for Jimi, other events were indicative of a final tailspin. As far back as 1968 Jimi, Noel and Mitch had attempted to separate themselves financially from Jeffrey, requesting that the record company pay the royalties direct to them but nothing had happened. For the most part, however, Jimi never really concerned himself with money. Whenever he wanted it, he simply asked. John Storyk recalls: "I never saw Jimi wear pants with pockets. I don't think he ever carried any money, there was always somebody there to pick it up. I don't think he even had a driver's licence." Michael Goldstein, a former press agent for Jeffrey, remembers that "Jimi would call up Mo Ostin [president of Warner Brothers] and say, 'I need ten Gs' and Mos would say, 'How do you want it?'" Even Jimi's notorious generosity, mostly to women, didn't really go beyond pocket money as far as Jeffrey was concerned.

In many ways, Michael Jeffrey had been crucial to Jimi's ascendancy, first with Chas Chandler and then on his own. There was no disputing that Jimi had become every inch a star, as Chandler and

(previous page)
Atlanta Pop Festival, Georgia, 4th July 1970.

photos: Joseph Sia

Jimi and road manager Eric Barrett arrive at Heathrow on 27th August 1970 *en route* **to the Isle of Wight Festival.**

Jeffrey had promised him, and he could have any material possession he wanted. However, Storyk notes: "I don't believe he had any interest in owning anything. He had some clothes and guitars, but I don't think he needed anything else." Still, he could fault management on a number of counts: firstly, they had permitted the Ed Chaplin suit to force a record (*Band Of Gypsies*) out of Jimi that he would rather not have released, and Chalpin was still pressing his suit in England where it was likely to cost Jimi even more money. Secondly, Michael Jeffrey had demanded that Jimi persist in a musical direction he had clearly outgrown and kept him on the road to pay for and maintain Electric Lady, Sgt. Pepper (Jeffrey's club in Majorca), and other expensive Jeffrey habits. Finally, Michael Jeffrey provided none of the understanding and guidance that Chas Chandler had, and Jimi felt increasingly isolated, with no advice or feedback to rely on. Claire Moeriece felt they "yessed him to death."

Although exhausted from the intensive rush of studio work and the mounting stress of business problems, Jimi was greatly looking forward to returning to England. The night before Jimi's arrival on August 27th had seen Electric Lady's official opening party, a Sixties-style rock 'n' roll blowout, and he and equipment manager Eric Barrett had not slept for at least a day. A good deal of attention was focussed on Jimi. He had not made a public appearance in England for over a year and a half and the press, old friends, and the whole London music scene were anxious to spend time with him.

In an interview with *The Times*, Jimi said: "I'm tired. Not physically. Mentally. I'm going to grow my hair back, it's something to hide behind." (Jimi's hair had been falling out because for years he had been perming it to straighten it. At the end of '69 he decided to cut it short and grow it out naturally.) But the three days between his arrival and the Isle of Wight concert were certainly not restful. He was besieged by the European press and London friends.

The Isle of Wight was not a lustrous return. The cumulative effects of fatigue and technical problems resulted in a sloppy, listless set, but there was no time to regroup. Jimi, Mitch, and Billy were booked for a quick sortie into Scandinavia and West Germany, then back through England.

None of it went very well. As Tom Edmunston, who had been one of the road managers on an earlier tour (for the Soft Machine) describes it: "He'd finish at around two in the morning, but he didn't get off his edge until six. He'd have another plane to catch at ten, so then he was on the plane until three, and at three, he had an interview, and then he was at the hotel and then he went for a sound check, and . . . then there was the show, and the same thing repeated itself. He didn't know how to get off it."

The tour was abruptly cancelled when Billy Cox, a non-indulger, was given a potent dose of acid that left him almost catatonic for days. Jimi, concerned for his old friend and relieved to be off the tour, took Billy back to London to find an out-of-the-way flat where he could recuperate. The whole situation was kept out of the papers.

That September London was full of Jimi's friends and enemies. Pat Hartley (whom Jimi had met in Hawaii) was there, Alan and Stella Douglas were there, Jeannette Jacobs was in town, along with Eric Burdon (fronting his hot new funky band, War), and Monika Danneman. (Monika and Jimi had met in January 1969 and had become secretly engaged in the March of that year.) Ed Chalpin was also on the scene, pressing his suit against Jimi in the English courts.

Waiting for a lift to the Isle of Wight.

A meeting was scheduled for the evening of September 15th, in order to deal with Jimi's complicated legal position. Representatives of all interested parties, including Track and Polydor Records and Chalpin were present but Jimi decided not to attend.

Later that same evening Jimi and Monika went to Ronnie Scott's to see War but left before the set. The next night he did jam with War, but appears to have played mostly rhythm guitar, although Burdon later told *Rolling Stone*: "He really got into *Tobacco Road*."

After the session Jimi and Monika went on to the Speakeasy for a meal then returned home. Most of the afternoon of 17th was spent shopping in Kensington and Chelsea where Jimi bumped into some people he knew from New York and announced to them that Monika and he were to be married the next month in Germany. (Up till then only Monika's family and Al Hendrix knew of the inpending wedding.) Later that afternoon he rang Henry Steingarten, his attorney in New York, to tell him that he was resolved to end his affiliation with Jeffrey and that he would be coming over to sort matters out.

The early part of the evening Monika and Jimi spent alone at their flat at the Hotel Samarkand and around 11 p.m. he wrote what was to be his last poem which he gave to her.

Around 2 a.m. on the morning of 18th, Monika drove Jimi to a flat belonging to Peter Cameron where Devon Wilson, Stella Douglas and Angie Burdon were also present. Monika dropped Jimi off and

I.o.W. Festival

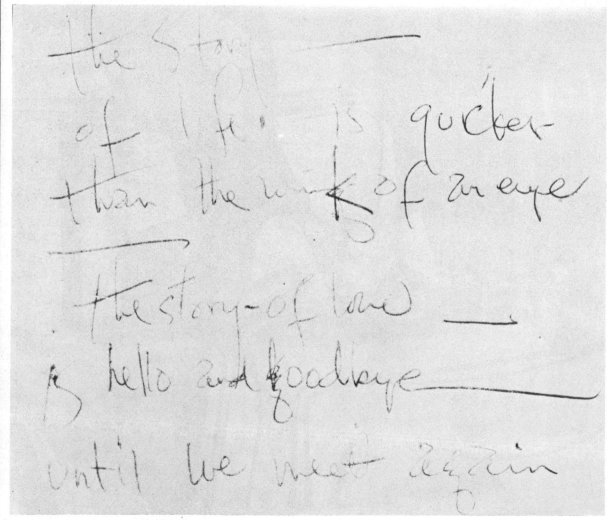

A snatch of Hendrix's last poem.

Photos: Pictorial Parade

Monika Danneman leaving the inquest.

came back to collect him half an hour later. They then returned to the Samarkand.

At about 7 a.m., Monika took a sleeping pill and fell asleep in Jimi's arms but awakened again at 10.20 a.m. She said at the inquest: "I couldn't sleep any more. I wanted some cigarettes, but as Jimi didn't like me going out without telling him, I looked to see if he was awake. He was sleeping normally. I went out to get some cigarettes for us and when I came back I looked at him again and there was sick on his nose and mouth. I tried to wake him up, but couldn't. Then I saw that he has taken some of my sleeping pills."

Monika tried to wake him up: "I shook him again and called his name but he did not wake up."

She called a girlfriend who was staying with Eric Burdon to see if she knew a private doctor who could come round immediately. Unfortunately she didn't and Monika called an ambulance instead. The ambulance arrived and one of the ambulance men took Jimi's pulse, checked his heart rate and looked at his eyes declaring that, in his opinion, Jimi would be OK to leave hospital that afternoon after a thorough checkup and Monika was not to worry. She then accompanied Jimi in the ambulance where he was sat up rather than being laid down which is apparently what should have happened. Indeed one of the ambulance men kept pushing Jimi's head back rather than letting him lean forward to vomit. Had he not done so the chances of Jimi surviving would have far been greater. As the ambulance entered the hospital gates minutes before 11.30 a.m. Jimi was given an oxygen mask to help his breathing but still Monika was

Hotel Samarkand, West London.

Kay Rowley

not unduly perturbed. Only when a nurse came to tell her that Jimi's heart had stopped but had started again did she realise how serious Jimi's condition was. A half an hour later at a few minutes past midday Monika was told that Jimi was dead.

The English coroner stated the cause of death as "inhalation of vomit and barbiturate intoxication," but returned an open verdict, declaring that there was "insufficient evidence of circumstances." *Rolling Stone* reported that pathologist Donald Teare told the inquest, "There were no signs of drug addiction."

Jimi's death was marked with the same kind of contradictions that marked his life. Since early reports implied that he had died of an overdose, this piece of misinformation was widely seized upon and led to the still-prevalent impression that he was an addict. Other obituaries were more respectful. The *New York Times*, for example, stated that his ". . . passionate, intense guitar playing stirred millions" and suggested that he was undergoing "inner turmoil." Carman Moore, in the *Village Voice*, wrote: ". . . if you could dig it, he was telling a billion frightened worshippers to go ahead and call what was beautiful, beautiful . . . Seize your life. A fuse in the new world, love machine, had gone out and cannot be replaced."

Jimi's music had always been full of intimations of death; now, to some, they seemed to have been a purposeful foreshadowing. In *Voodoo Chile*, he says: "If I don't meet you no more in this world, I'll meet you in the next one . . . Don't be late," and *Angel*, recorded in August, also incorporates some eerie lines about death and its heavenly aftermath.

97

(left) Jimi's coffin followed by
his brother Leon and his
father Al.
(right) Devon Wilson and
Alan Douglas at the funeral.

Jim Marshall

Eric Burdon read the poem Jimi wrote the night before he
died and claimed that it was a "suicide note." Burdon told the BBC
three days later that "he used a drug to phase himself out of this life
and go someplace else." He also strongly implied that Michael Jeffrey
(who had been Burdon's manager when he was with the Animals,
and who Burdon was suing for misappropriating funds) had been
siphoning off huge amounts of Jimi's earnings.

This insinuation dovetailed with another theory that began to
circulate — that Hendrix had been murdered. It was widely felt that
the imminent expiration of Jimi's management contract with Jeffrey
and his failure to put out new product for over a year, combined
with the escalating cost of Electric Lady, had made Jimi a commodity
worth more dead than alive. Although there is much evidence to
suggest that the business affairs of Jeffrey and Yameta, a Bahamian
holding company formed to manage Jimi's money, were conducted
in an irregular fashion, the murder theories, along with the
suggestion that Jimi had been done away with by Mafia lords,
angered because Electric Lady had been built in their domain
(Greenwich Village) without dues being paid, are nothing more than
flimsy, unsubstantiated rumors.

Jeffrey was in attendance on October 1, at Jimi's funeral in Seattle.
Also present were Mitch and Noel, Alan Douglas, Johnny Winter,
John Hammond, Jr., Buddy Miles, Miles Davis, Steve Paul and Eddie
Kramer. The service itself was a somber and dignified affair, the tone
set by Al Hendrix and other members of Jimi's family. Spirituals were
the only music. A memorial concert of festival proportions was,
according to *Rolling Stone*, scratched, "partly due to lack of time to
properly organize it, and partly because the city of Seattle freaked at
the idea. 'If we can't do it right, we won't do it at all,' Jimi's father
said . . ."

In 1969, Jimi had told the *New York Times*: "I tell you, when I die,
I'm not going to have a funeral, I'm going to have a jam session."
He was half right. The jam session after the funeral went on for some
hours, the musicians paying tributes to Jimi in the way he wanted,
by playing music.

99

Among the pall bearers at Jimi's funeral were his valet, Herbert Price (left), Donny Howell (behind him) and Eddie Rye (front right) friends from the Seattle days.

Mitch and Noel at the jam after the funeral.

The tangled mess of Jimi's business affairs and finances and the voluminous legacy of unfinished or unmixed tapes he left behind gave rise to one of rock's uglier chapters, as a rat's nest of greed and exploitation emerged during the Seventies.

Michael Jeffrey was one of the first of the "modern" rock managers. In the late Sixties rock 'n' roll was still a frontier enterprise and Jeffrey had an entrepreneural style ideally suited to the free-wheeling nature of a business that grew too fast. Tom Edmunston, who managed the Soft Machine for Michael Jeffrey and who was a force on the New York rock scene in 1969–70, remembers that Jeffrey was ". . . a brilliant guy, who had been a counter-intelligence agent for MI-5. He was a myopic person of a highly critical paranoid intelligence. He had a habit of disappearing for days and letting other people function, and having everyone get mad at him, and the madder they got, the more power, abstract power, he got."

Jeffrey's management tactics were insensitive at best, unsavory at worst. At one point, Jimi told Claire Moeriece that he had been kidnapped. Clare: "Yeah, and his management came and mysteriously stopped them [the kidnappers] and kept him from being beaten up. They just happened to come by at the right time, at some warehouse." She felt that "management", often in the guise of undesirable and dangerous people she declined to name, had attempted to solidify Jimi's dependence by this staged abduction.

Edmunston reports several occasions on which huge amounts of money went missing: "During the 'British Are Coming' tour, Jerry Stickells and I would collect the money and we'd have 120, 60, 80 thousand dollars. We'd wire it back to New York. When we got back there was a discrepancy of like $80,000. I told Jeffrey and Jeffrey and Steve Weiss [Jeffrey's lawyer] said, 'Forget about it.'"

Shortly after Jimi died, Jeffrey told Al Hendrix that Jimi's estate would amount to $21,000, the cash he had on him at the time of his death. Jimi's lawyer, Henry Steingarten, was a partner of Jeffrey's lawyer, Steve Weiss. A *Rolling Stone* article on December 2, 1976, reports that through working out various open questions – selling Jimi's share of Electric Lady to Jeffrey for $240,000, the successful resolution of the Chalpin suits in England (for which Chalpin had to pay $150,000 in court costs) and the sale of rights to previously unreleased material (which resulted in the "Alan Douglas albums") – the value of the estate increased to two million dollars. Al Hendrix also engaged a lawyer, Leo Branton, who forced Henry Steingarten to resign as administrator of Jimi's estate under threat of conflict of interest charges.

Branton never reached the bottom of the Yameta scam, however, the Bahamian holding corporation set up to protect Michael Jeffrey and his partners, shadowy English financiers, from tax liability. Warner Brothers sent Jimi's royalty checks there, as well as Mitch's and Noel's (who later sued and won $100,000 and $300,000, respectively, for withheld royalties). It is likely that much of Michael Jeffrey's half of the Electric Lady costs came out of Yameta, as well as funding for Sgt. Pepper's, the club he owned on Majorca. It is also likely, according to Jerry Hopkins in *Rolling Stone*, that "upwards of one million dollars gushed into the account, and that all of it gurgled out without one immediately apparent penny ever going to anyone in the Jimi Hendrix Experience."

Everyone connected with Yameta stonewalled Hopkins and other investigators. Certainly, little more will be learned about Michael

Jim Marshall

Jeffrey's unorthodox fiscal dealings since he died in a plane crash over Majorca in 1972 (also felt by some to have been in suspicious circumstances).

Since Jimi had little use for money beyond the cost of guitars (and related equipment) and his libidinal taste for self-indulgence, the onus of disentangling these questionable practices fell upon his estate and Al Hendrix. Leo Branton remedied the situation for Al, although he also fell prey to a phony Jimi Hendrix Memorial Foundation scam, run by some Seattle hustlers.

Far more grave, in terms of its ultimate ramifications, was the posthumous release of several Jimi Hendrix albums, culled and assembled from the hundreds (Alan Douglas estimated 600) of hours of studio and live tapes. The difficulty with the posthumous albums was that they were completed by people trying to convey what they believed Jimi had in mind. Like works of fine art finished by disciples after a master has died, they may impart the form and style of the creator, but are, at best, only renderings of the artist's substance and imagination. The most serious liability in this case, in addition to purveying material that was simply never completed, lies in Jimi's absence from a critical stage of the process – the mix. Although Eddie Kramer had an acute sense of Jimi's aural aesthetic, their work together was a fertile collaboration and Jimi's death aborted its productive energy. Also, Jimi was still learning the capabilities of the studio as a tool and still expanding his vision as a producer.

Still, the first albums particularly, *Cry of Love* and *Rainbow Bridge*, have a feeling of near-authenticity. This material was closest to completion at the time of his death, containing songs that Jimi had earmarked for the *First Rays Of The New Rising Sun* set. Both albums, which Kramer finished with Mitch's assistance, offer evidence of a logical progression (with a healthy dollop of surprise), within the framework of an already-established Hendrix style. *Pali Gap* (from *Rainbow Bridge*) and *Drifting* (*Cry of Love*) exemplify Jimi's more exploratory/astral/sound-sculpture direction, primarily instrumental and dense, almost lush, with multi-tracked guitars and an evocative, personal point of view. This side of Jimi, in these songs as well as *Hey, Baby, Land Of The New Rising Sun*, and *My Friend*, achieve a kind of beauty that the more cosmic tracks on *Electric Ladyland* were approaching. On the newer songs, Jimi's guitar is seamlessly woven into the body of the music. He plays less against the music, as if he had finally resolved at least one conflict – he could "play pretty" if he wanted.

Other pieces, like *Earth Blues* (*Rainbow Bridge*) and *Freedom* (*Cry Of Love*), extend Jimi's developing theme of universal love. *Earth Blues* features the Ronettes with whom Jimi sets up a snappy call and response.

Perhaps the best-known song from these albums is Jimi's sardonic paean to Devon Wilson, *Dolly Dagger*. It deftly demonstrates Devon's power and sensuality as a woman ("Here comes Dolly Dagger, her love's so strong, gonna make you stagger") but also contained a prophetic warning that her drug habit would destroy her. Like Michael Jeffrey, Devon crashed shortly after Jimi's death. seriously addicted, she fell, jumped (or was pushed?) from an upper storey of New York's Chelsea Hotel.

War Heroes and *Hendrix In The West* are less successful, the *Village Voice* calling Jimi's performance on *War Heroes* "stumbling and enervated." Nonetheless, there are interesting cuts on these albums, even though both were attempts by Michael Jeffrey to squeeze yet another record out of unfinished or inferior Hendrix tapes. *Hendrix In The West*, at le st, contains Jimi's flashy and exuberant version of *Johnny B. Goode* from the Berkeley concerts. You can almost hear him duck walk.

In 1974, Alan Douglas finally realized his desire to produce Jimi Hendrix. Warner Brothers turned over to Douglas about five hundred hours of tapes in the hope he could sift through them and extract more releasable product. These tapes had not been accessible to Michael Jeffrey and contained material Jimi had recorded at the Record Plant in 1969 and '70, and at Electric Lady during his last months. According to a *Village Voice* article, dated August 29, 1974: "The tapes fall roughly into three categories: some dazzling free-form jams, with jazz-oriented musicians, like [John] McLaughlin and organist Larry Young; jams with less cerebral types – Johnny Winter, Stephen Stills, Eric Clapton, Traffic, and others, most of which is pretty, but not exactly mind-boggling; and finally, blues and R&B-based music, some of it loosened-up versions of previously-recorded tracks, but mostly new material, with a wild, loose, beautifully funky feel. . .". Douglas had overseen the original McLaughlin sessions, and these, along with Jimi's announced plans to record with Gil Evans and a long dialogue between Jimi, Douglas and Miles Davis, form the basis for Douglas' contention that ". . . without question, he was leaning towards a jazz involvement. It would probably have turned out to be the original fusion records." Reportedly, neither Warner Brothers nor McLaughlin were anxious to release the jams, believing them to be too rough, and they never saw the light of day.

Alan Douglas took an unusual approach to the rest of the material. He decided to wipe the backing track, eliminating Mitch, Noel, Billy Cox and Buddy Miles, and re-record the songs, keeping Jimi's guitars and vocals and adding studio musicians dubbed behind him. The results were *Crash Landing* and *Midnight Lightning*, which Warner Brothers released in 1974 and '75. Many critics felt they were a desecration, although they sold reasonably well. Critic Dave Marsh called them ". . . abominations unto the Lord" and, indeed, they have a flawed, awkward and strained feeling to them. Completely lacking in spontaneity, they sound like the patchwork records they are: on the one hand Jimi – raw and inspired in 1969 – and on the other, self-conscious studio musicians trying to find a way into the music in 1974. They are not great contributions to the Hendrix oeuvre, but *The Essential Jimi Hendrix, Volumes 1 & 2* are valuable compilations, in which Alan Douglas distilled much of the best of early Hendrix and for which he wrote intelligent and insightful liner notes.

There are dozens of other Jimi Hendrix albums. Live recordings from The Jimi Hendrix Experience concerts in Europe and the US, bootlegs from loft jams, or nights at The Scene, scattered bits and pieces from almost-forgotten sessions with Little Richard, Arthur Lee (of Love), and Jim Morrison, the Woodstock albums, etc. Rarely has an artist's work been so mercilessly plundered. During his lifetime, there were five Jimi Hendrix albums, including *Smash Hits*, which was basically a greatest hits album. Today, there are over forty Jimi Hendrix records on the market, most of them containing music Hendrix would never have wanted heard. They do him a disservice.

There can be no facile summing up, no tidy denouement of the Jimi Hendrix story. Every component of his life spawned its own contradiction, its own schizophrenic pull and these polar personalities engaged in a perpetually dynamic tug-of-war. As his star ascended, the chasm widened until it could no longer sustain a life. Perhaps the growing distance was between Jimmy and Jimi. Jimmy was a shy boy, deeply in need of an absent mother's love, who sought comfort and identity in music; Jimi was a conscious superstar, who, though revelling in the transient adulation of millions, became trapped by the music business.

Other dichotomies abound. Jimi saw himself as a cosmic messenger communicating his awareness of 'the other side' through his music. The public tended to see him as the high priest of free love who achieved lasting intimacy only with his guitar. His music preached freedom and change, but he was forced to re-cover ground he has already explored, hindering his own growth as an artist. Both vilified and lionized from the beginning, Jimi was often regarded as a decadent devil, though, ironically, he was never able to conquer his own internal demons. For a time, Jimi was thought an unfortunate exponent of bombastic, psychedelic overstatement and his lyrics were often seen as banal excess, rather than high fantastical poetry.

Critical hindsight of the Seventies tends to label Jimi as a pathetic victim of the music machine, rather than a cosmic musical trail-blazer. Jimi Hendrix was an original genius, whose like had never been seen before or since. He single-handedly defined the electric guitar as a modern musical instrument and was well on his way towards doing the same for the technological innovations of studio production. His alchemist's touch is felt today in his influence on other experimental musicians, such as John McLaughlin, Robin Trower and Robert Fripp. Perceptive conceptions of what music could be were altered by his space-sound insinuations. Finally, though Hendrix can be seen in Jungian terms as a shadow archetype, an emissary of darkness on to which narrow minds project the army of their own fears, he exercised a significantly more positive effect in creating the first musical bridge between black R&B and white rock 'n' roll, a bridge which many have since crossed.

Jimi Hendrix was the first sacrifice of the Sixties to its own dark rituals. Although he was victimized, he was not wholly a victim, since he did get what he wanted and he helped create the instruments of his own destruction. After his entry into the Pantheon of rockdom, he was always on the edge, in a place no one else ever visited, let alone staked out as home territory. In the end, the greatest tragedy of his death is that he was so far ahead of his time. If he could have waited, the world would have somehow caught up and known better how to deal with him.

The experience of Jimi occurred before there was a methodology of protection for stars of his lustre. If he were to appear now and assuming his genius — born, perhaps, of madness — would be recognized, there would be more supervision and guidance, since he apparently couldn't, or wouldn't, take care of himself. Hendrix was not a martyr; he made choices and opted to ignore, at least outwardly, the dangerous currents swirling about him. The desperation that compelled him to act as destructively as he did might well have softened had he been able to answer the questions he asked himself. Then there might have been shelter and rest within the path he chose.

During his lifetime Jimi Hendrix sanctioned the release of five albums, one of which was a compilation of hit singles and favored LP tracks. Since his death that figure has swelled to an indeterminate number (at least 50), making Hendrix one of the most prolific recording artists in the world, at least on paper. But the huge number of Hendrix LPs to be found in the racks on any large record store belies the fact that no other artist has had his reject barrel plundered so thoroughly as Hendrix. Most of the material is sub-standard, boring and grossly exploitative.

The posthumous releases fall into four distinct categories:

a) Re-issues. The "official" Hendrix material from the four studio albums recorded between 1967 and 1970 (*Are You Experienced?*, *Axis: Bold As Love*, *Electric Ladyland* and *Cry Of Love*) has been repackaged ad infinitum by Polydor (or Warner Brothers in the US) to the extent that duplications, and duplications of duplications, abound like rabbits all around the globe. Different combinations of the same tracks litter the 19 albums on the current UK Polydor catalogue.

b) Pre-1966 material. Before Hendrix was brought to London in 1966, he recorded with various American artists, always in a subordinate capacity or simply jamming in the studio while the tape was running. Records with (or indeed *by*) the Isley Brothers, Curtis Knight, Little Richard and Lonnie Youngblood fall into this category, as do the *Jimi Hendrix At His Best* trilogy (a gross misnomer) and most albums with the word "roots" somewhere in the title. Many of these tapes have been leased by the producer to several different labels over the years with the result that the same titles crop up again and again.

c) Post-1966 material and jams. Hendrix loved to play, whether it was on stage, in the studio or in someone's front room, and he never seemed to care whether a tape recorder was running. Again much of this material is poor quality, but American producer Alan Douglas assembled a series of albums from such studio out-takes during the Seventies with the sanction of the Hendrix estate and the "official" record companies (Polydor and Warner Brothers). These offer a higher quality of material than anything in category (b) but would never have seen the light of day had Hendrix lived.

d) Live. Many Hendrix concerts were recorded, presumably for personal use at the time, only to find their way on to official records during the Seventies. The quality varies considerably and it is doubtful whether most of these would have been released had Hendrix lived. The CBS double set *The Jimi Hendrix Concerts*, released in 1982, is the best of the bunch.

The following discography is as comprehensive as any listing yet published but, because of the wholesale confusion that exists over re-issues on so many different labels, there are probably a few omissions. As a general rule, the material on Polydor (Warner Brothers in the US) represents the best of Hendrix's work despite the numerous duplications. The cream appears on the four studio LPs originally released by Track Records in the UK.

Additional Notes

1. Disputed producer credits are rife within the Hendrix catalogue. According to Chas Chandler, Eddie Kramer was employed as the engineer on Hendrix's first three albums and not as producer. Chandler produced both *Are You Experienced?* and *Axis: Bold As Love*

and about half the tracks on *Electric Ladyland*. The other half of this double set was produced by Hendrix himself with Kramer's assistance.

2. Most large city record shops offer a range of Hendrix albums imported from abroad, usually from France, Germany or Japan. Track listings may vary slightly on these albums but the actual music itself is covered within the discography.

3. In September 1974 the British Budget label Music For Pleasure released a Hendrix album called *The Birth Of Success* (Cat. No. MfP 50053). Long since deleted, a track listing is presently unavailable.

4. Polydor Records have made available a 12 record boxed set entitled the *10th Anniversary Box*. These albums contain all the material to be found within the Polydor copyright including posthumous material produced by Alan Douglas.

Singles (UK)

Date	Title	Label	Cat. No.
Dec 1966	Hey Joe/Stone Free	Polydor	56 139
Mar 1967	Purple Haze/51st Anniversary	Track	604 001
May 1967	The Wind Cries Mary/Highway Chile	Track	604 004
Aug 1967	The Burning Of The Midnight Lamp/The Stars That Play With Laughing Sam's Dice	Track	604 007
Sep 1967	How Would You Feel/You Don't Want Me (with Curtis Knight)	Track	604 009
Oct 1967	Hush Now/Flashing (with Curtis Knight)	London	HL 10160
Oct 1968	All Along The Watchtower/Long Hot Summer Night	Track	604 025
Apr 1969	Crosstown Traffic/Gypsy Eyes	Track	604 029
Oct 1969	(Let Me Light Your) Fire/Burning Of The Midnight Lamp	Track	604 033
Oct 1970	Voodoo Chile/Hey Joe/All Along The Watchtower	Track	2095 001
Oct 1970	Ballad of Jimi/Gloomy Monday (with Curtis Knight)	London	HL 10321
Dec 1970	No Such Animal Pt 1/No Such Animal Pt 2 (with Curtis Knight)	RCA	2033
Apr 1971	Angel/Night Bird Flying	Track	2094 007
Jan 1972	Johnny B. Goode/Little Wing	Polydor	2001 277
1973	Hear My Train A'Coming/Rock Me Baby	Reprise	K 14286
1978	Gloria/(One sided single with album 2612 034 — *The Essential Jimi Hendrix*)	Polydor	JIMI 1
Sep 1980	Hey Joe/Stone Free (re-issue)	Polydor	2141 275
Sep 1980	Purple Haze/51st Anniversary (re-issue)	Polydor	2141 276
Sep 1980	The Wind Cries Mary (re-issue)	Polydor	2141 277
Sep 1980	The Burning Of The Midnight Lamp/The Stars That Play With Laughing Sam's Dice (re-issue)	Polydor	2141 278
Sep 1980	All Along The Watchtower/Long Hot Summer Night (re-issue)	Polydor	2141 279
Sep 1980	Voodoo Chile/Gloria (re-issue)	Polydor	2141 280
Sep 1980	(All above six singles in boxed set)	Polydor	260 8001

EPs (UK)

Date	Title		Label	Cat. No.
Oct 1971	Gypsy Eyes/Remember/Purple Haze/Stone Free		Track	2094 010
Dec 1981	All Along The Watchtower/Foxy Lady/Purple Haze/ Manic Depression		Polydor	POSPX 401

Title

ARE YOU EXPERIENCED?

Tracks
Foxy Lady, Manic Depression, Red House, Can You See Me, Love Or Confusion, I Don't Live Today, May This Be Love, Fire, Third Stone From The Sun, Remember, Are You Experienced.
Personnel
Jimi Hendrix (guitar, vocals), Noel Redding (bass), Mitch Mitchell (drums).
Producer
Chas Chandler
Original Release Date
May, 1967
Label & Catalogue No.
Track 612/613 001. Re-issued November 1970 as Track 2407 010. Currently available as double album with "Axis: Bold As Love", Polydor 2683 031 (released October 1973) or Polydor 613 001 (re-issued November, 1981) USA: Warner Reprise 6261.
Note: The track listing on the US version of this album differed Depression, Hey Joe, Love Or Confusion, May This Be Love, I Don't Live Today, The Wind Cries Mary, Fire, Third Stone From The Sun, Today, The Wind Cries Mary, Fire, Third Stone From The Sun, Foxy Lady, Are You Experienced.

Title

AXIS: BOLD AS LOVE

Tracks
EXP, Up From The Skies, Spanish Castle Magic, Wait Until Tomorrow, Ain't No Telling, Little Wing, If Six Was Nine, You've Got Me Floating, Castles Made Of Sand, She's So Fine, One Rainy Wish, Little Miss Lover, Bold As Love.
Personnel
Jimi Hendrix (guitar, vocals), Noel Redding (bass), Mitch Mitchell (drums)
Producer
Chas Chandler
Original Release Date
November, 1967
Label & Catalogue No.
Track 612/613 003. Re-issued in November, 1970, as Track 2407 011. Currently available as double album with Are You Experienced?, Polydor 2683 031. USA: Warner Reprise 6281.

Title

GET THAT FEELING (with Curtis Knight)

Tracks
How Would You Feel, Gloomy Monday, Get That Feeling, Hush Now, Hornet's Nest, Strange Things, Odd Ball, Day Tripper.
Personnel
Jimi Hendrix (guitar), Curtis Knight (vocals) plus others.
Producer
Ed Chalpin
Original Release date
February, 1968
Label & Catalogue No.
London HA/SH 8349.

Title

SMASH HITS

Tracks
Purple Haze, The Wind Cries Mary, Can You See Me, 51st Anniversary, Hey Joe, Stone Free, The Stars That Play With Laughing Sam's Dice, Manic Depression, Highway Chile, The Burning Of The Midnight Lamp, Foxy Lady.
Personnel
Various (compilation album).
Producer
Chas Chandler
Original Release Date
April, 1968
Label & Catalogue No.
Track 612/613 004. Re-issued in June, 1973, as Polydor 2310 268.
USA: Warner Reprise K 2276.

Title

ELECTRIC LADYLAND

Tracks
And The Gods Made Love, Have You Ever Been To Electric Ladyland, Crosstown Traffic, Voodoo Chile, Little Miss Strange, Long Hot Summer Night, Come On (Part One), Gypsy Eyes, Burning Of The Midnight Lamp, Rainy Day Dream Away, 1983 (A Merman I Should Turn To Be), Moon Turn The Tides Gently Gently Away, Still Raining Still Dreaming, House Burning Down, All Along The Watchtower, Voodoo Chile (Slight Return).
Personnel
Jimi Hendrix (guitar, vocals), Jack Cassady (bass), Mitch Mitchell, Buddy Miles (drums), Steve Winwood (organ), Al Kooper (piano), Chris Wood (flute), Mike Finnegan (organ), Freddie Smith (reeds), Larry Faucette (congas).
Producers
Jimi Hendrix, Chas Chandler (certain tracks only)'
Original Release Date
October, 1968

Label & Catalogue No.
Track 613 008/9. Re-issued one year after release as two separate albums. Track 613 010 (Part 1) and Track 613 017 (Part 2). Re-issued in June, 1973, as Polydor 2657 012 and also as two separate albums, Polydor 2310 271 (Part 1) and Polydor 2310 272 (Part 2). USA: Warner Reprise 6307.

Title

STRANGE THINGS (with Curtis Knight)

Tracks
Unknown
Personnel
Jimi Hendrix (guitar, vocals), Curtis Knight (vocals) plus others.
Producer
Ed Chalpin
Original Release Date
November, 1968
Label & Catalogue No.
London HA/SH 8369

Title

BACKTRACK 1

Tracks
Hey Joe, Wind Cries Mary (various other Track artists appear on album).
Personnel
Jimi Hendrix (guitar, vocals), Noel Redding (bass), Mitch Mitchell (drums).
Producer
Chas Chandler
Original Release Date
May, 1970
Label & Catalogue No.
Track 2407 001

Title

BACKTRACK 2

Tracks
Purple Haze, Let Me Light Your Fire (various other Track artists appear on album).
Personnel
Jimi Hendrix (guitar, vocals), Noel Redding (bass), Mitch Mitchell (drums).
Producer
Chas Chandler
Original Release Date
May, 1970
Label & Catalogue No.
Track 2407 002

Title

BACKTRACK 3: WHO AND HENDRIX

Tracks
Hey Joe, I Don't Live Today, Purple Haze, Can You See Me, The Wind
Cries Mary, Stone Free. (These tracks occupy side two; seven Who
tracks occupy side one).
Personnel
Jimi Hendrix (guitar, vocals), Noel Redding (bass), Mitch Mitchell
(drums).
Producer
Chas Chandler
Original Release Date
May, 1970
Label & Catalogue No.
Track 2407 003

Title

BACKTRACK 4: WHO AND HENDRIX
(with The Who)

Tracks
Burning Of The Midnight Lamp, Are You Experienced, If Six Was
Nine, Remember, Gypsy Eyes, All Along The Watchtower. (These
tracks occupy side two; six Who tracks occupy side one).
Personnel
Jimi Hendrix (guitar, vocals), Noel Redding (bass), Mitch Mitchell
(drums).
Producer
Chas Chandler
Original Release Date
May, 1970
Label & Catalogue No.
Track 2407 004

Title

BACKTRACK 5: WHO AND HENDRIX
(with The Who)

Tracks
Rainy Day Dream Away, Manic Depression, Love Or Confusion,
Come On, Spanish Castle Magic, Voodoo Chile (Slight Return). (These
tracks occupy side two; seven Who tracks occupy side one).
Personnel
Jimi Hendrix (guitar, vocals), Noel Redding (bass), Mitch Mitchell
(drums).
Producer
Chas Chandler
Original Release Date
May, 1970
Label & Catalogue No.
Track 2407 005.

Title

BAND OF GYPSIES

Tracks
Who Knows, Machine Gun, Changes, Power To Love, Message Of Love, We Gotta Live Together.
Personnel
Jimi Hendrix (guitar, vocals), Billy Cox (bass), Buddy Miles (drums).
Producer
Jimi Hendrix
Original Release Date
June, 1970
Label & Catalogue No.
Track 2406 002. Re-issued in June, 1973, as Polydor 2480 005.
USA: Capitol STAO 472.
Note: Recorded live at the Fillmore East, New York, on New Year's Eve, 1970.

Title

BACKTRACK 7

Tracks
How Would You Feel (with Curtis Knight), Long Hot Summer Night, The Stars That Play With Laughing Sam's Dice. (Various other Track artists appear on album).
Personnel
Jimi Hendrix (guitar, vocals), Noel Redding (bass), Mitch Mitchell (drums); plus Curtis Knight (vocals).
Producers
Jimi Hendrix, Chas Chandler, Curtis Knight.
Original Release Date
November, 1970
Label & Catalogue No.
Track 2407 007

Title

WOODSTOCK

Tracks
Star Spangled Banner, Purple Haze (on three album set with various other artists).
Personnel
Jimi Hendrix (guitar, vocals), Billy Cox (bass), Mitch Mitchell (drums).
Producer

Original Release Date
1970
Label & Catalogue No.
Polydor 2402 003
Note: Recorded live at Woodstock Festival, August, 1969.

Title

THE CRY OF LOVE

Tracks
Freedom, Drifting, Ezy Rider, Night Bird Flying, My Friend, Straight
Ahead, Astro Man, Angel, In From The Storm, Belly Button Window.
Personnel
Jimi Hendrix (guitar, vocals), Billy Cox (bass), Mitch Mitchell (drums);
also Buddy Miles (drums, Ezy Rider), Buzzy Linhart (vibes, Drifting),
Steve Winwood and Chris Wood (vibes, Drifting).
Producers
Jimi Hendrix, Eddie Kramer.
Original Release Date
March, 1971
Label & Catalogue No.
Track 2408 101. Re-issued by Polydor in June, 1973, as Polydor
2302 023. USA: Warner Reprise MS 2034.

Title

THE ETERNAL FIRE OF JIMI HENDRIX
(with Curtis Knight)

Tracks
How Would You Feel, Love Love, Hush Now, Flashing, Day Tripper
(Part 1), You Don't Want Me, Hush Now (instr), Simon Says, Level,
Love Love.
Personnel
Jimi Hendrix (guitar, vocals), Curtis Knight.
Producer
Ed Chalpin
Original Release Date
April, 1971
Label & Catalogue No.
Hallmark SHM 732

Title

EXPERIENCE (Original Soundtrack)

Tracks
Sunshine Of Your Love, Room Full Of Mirrors, Bleeding Heart,
Smashing Of Amps.
Personnel
Jimi Hendrix (guitar, vocals), Noel Redding (bass), Mitch Mitchell
(drums).
Producers
Steve Gold, Michael Jeffrey.
Original Release Date
August, 1971
Label & Catalogue No.
Ember NR 5057. Subsequently re-issued by Bulldog Records as
BDL 4002 in 1979.
Note: Recorded live at Albert Hall, London, on February 18, 1969.

LIVE AT THE ISLE OF WIGHT

Tracks
Midnight Lightning, Foxy Lady, Lover Man, Freedom, All Along The Watchtower, In From The Storm.
Personnel
Jimi Hendrix (guitar, vocals), Billy Cox (bass), Mitch Mitchell (drums).
Producer
Michael Jeffrey (executive).
Original Release Date
November, 1971
Label & Catalogue No.
Polydor 2302 016

Title

RAINBOW BRIDGE   (Original Soundtrack)

Tracks
Dolly Dagger, Earth Blues, Pali Gap, Room Full Of Mirrors, Star Spangled Banner, Look Over Yonder, Hear My Train A'Coming, Hey Baby.
Personnel
Jimi Hendrix (guitar, vocals), Billy Cox (bass), Mitch Mitchell, Buddy Miles (drums), Juma Edwards (percussion).
Producer
Eddie Kramer
Original Release Date
November, 1971
Label & Catalogue No.
Warner Reprise K 44159

Title

CLASSIC PERFORMANCES FROM THE MONTEREY POP FESTIVAL   (with Otis Redding)

Tracks
Hey Joe, Like A Rolling Stone, Rock Me Baby, Can You See Me, Wild Thing.
Personnel
Jimi Hendrix (guitar, vocals), Noel Redding (bass), Mitch Mitchell (drums).
Producer
Original Release Date
1971
Label & Catalogue No.
Warner Reprise K 40430

Title

HENDRIX IN THE WEST

Tracks
Blue Suede Shoes, Little Wing, Lover Man, The Queen, Red House,
Sgt. Pepper's Lonely Hearts Club Band, Voodoo Chile.
Personnel
Jimi Hendrix (guitar, vocals), Noel Redding and/or Billy Cox (bass),
Mitch Mitchell (drums).
Producer
Unknown
Original Release Date
February, 1972
Label & Catalogue No.
Polydor 2302 018
Note: Live tracks recorded at the Berkeley Community Centre,
California, Sports Arena, San Diego, California, The Isle of Wight
Festival (1970) and the Royal Albert Hall, London (1969).

Title

MORE EXPERIENCE

Tracks
Little Ivy, Voodoo Chile, Roomful Of Mirrors, Fire, Purple Haze,
Wild Thing, Bleeding Heart.
Musicians
Jimi Hendrix (guitar, vocals), Noel Redding (bass), Mitch Mitchell
(drums).
Producers
Steve Gold; Michael Jeffrey (executive).
Original Release Date
1972
Label & Catalogue No.
Ember NR 5061. Subsequently re-issued by Bulldog Records as
BDL 4003 in 1979.

Title

RARE HENDRIX

Tracks
Good Feeling, Voice In The Wind, Go Go Shoes, Go Go Shoes (Part 2),
Good Time, Bring My Baby Back, Suspicious, Hot Trigger.
Personnel
Jimi Hendrix (guitar, vocals), Lonnie Youngblood (reeds), Herman
Hitson (guitar), Lee Moses (guitar).
Producer
John Brantley
Original Release Date
November, 1972
Label & Catalogue No.
Enterprise ENTF 3000. Subsequently re-issued by Audio Fidelity
AFEMP 1016, September 1981, with re-arranged track order.

Title

WAR HEROES

Tracks
Bleeding Heart, Highway Chile, Tax Free, Peter Gunn, Catastrophe,
Stepping Stone, Midnight, Three Little Bears, Beginning, Izabclla.
Personnel
Jimi Hendrix (guitar, vocals), Billy Cox (bass), Mitch Mitchell (drums).
Producer
Unknown
Original Release Date
September, 1972
Label & Catalogue No.
Polydor 2302 020.

Title

JIMI HENDRIX AT HIS BEST VOL. 1

Tracks
She Went To Bed With My Guitar, Free Thunder, Cave Man Bells,
Strokin' A Lady On Each Hip, Baby Chicken Strut.
Personnel
Jimi Hendrix (guitar, vocals), Mike Ephron (occasional keyboards),
unidentified percussionist.
Producer
Mike Ephron
Original Release Date
1972
Label & Catalogue No.
Sagapan 6313.

Title

JIMI HENDRIX AT HIS BEST VOL. 2

Tracks
Down Mean Blues, Feel's Good, Fried Cola, Monday Morning Blues,
Jimi Is Tender Too, Madagascar.
Personnel
Jimi Hendrix (guitar, vocals), Mike Ephron (occasional keyboards),
unidentified percussionist.
Producer
Mike Ephron
Original Release Date
1972
Label & Catalogue No.
Sagapan 6314

Title

JIMI HENDRIX AT HIS BEST VOL. 3

Tracks
Young Jim, Lift Off, Swift's Wing, Spiked With Heady Dreams, Giraffe.
Personnel
Jimi Hendrix (guitar, vocals), Mike Ephron (occasional keyboards), unidentified percussionist.
Producer
Mike Ephron
Original Release Date
1972
Label & Catalogue No.
Sagapan 6315

Title

WOODSTOCK 2

Tracks
Jam Back At The House, Izabella, Got My Heart Back Together (on two-album set with various other artists).
Personnel
Jimi Hendrix (guitar, vocals), Billy Cox (bass), Mitch Mitchell (drums).
Producer
Unknown
Original Release Date
1972
Label & Catalogue No.
Polydor 2657 016
Note: Recorded live at Woodstock Festival, August, 1969.

Title

IN THE BEGINNING

Tracks
You Got Me Running, Money, Let's Go Let's Go Let's Go, You Got What It Takes, Sweet Little Angel, Walkin' The Dog, There's Something On Your Mind, Hard Night.
Personnel
Jimi Hendrix (guitar, vocals), Curtis Knight.
Producer
Ed Chalpin
Original Release Date
October, 1973
Label & Catalogue No.
Ember NR 5068
Note: Recorded live at Club 20, Hackensack, New Jersey, 1966.

Title

THE WILD ONE

Tracks
Get That Feeling, You Don't Want Me, Gloomy Monday, Happy
Birthday, Future Trip, Strange Things, Odd Ball (instrumental),
Welcome Home, Hornet's Nest (instrumental), How Would You Feel.
Personnel
Jimi Hendrix (guitar, vocals), Curtis Knight (vocals).
Producer
Ed Chalpin
Original Release Date
1973
Label & Catalogue No.
Hallmark SHM 791

Title

LOOSE ENDS

Tracks
Coming Down Hard On Me Baby, Blue Suede Shoes, Jam 292,
The Stars That Play With Laughing Sam's Dice, The Drifter's Escape,
Burning Desire, I'm Your Hoochie Coochie Man, Have You Ever Been
To Electric Ladyland
Personnel
Jimi Hendrix (guitar, vocals), Billy Cox (bass), Mitch Mitchell (drums),
Noel Redding (bass), Buddy Miles (drums).
Producer
Alex Turner
Original Release Date
February, 1974
Label & Catalogue No.
Polydor 2310 301

Title

LOOKING BACK WITH JIMI HENDRIX

Tracks
You Got Me Running, Money, Let's Go Let's Go Let's Go, You Got
What It Takes, Sweet Little Angel, Walk The Dog, There's Something
On Your Mind, Hard Night, Hush Now, Knock Yourself Out, Ballad Of
Jimi, No Business, Gotta Have A New Dress, Don't Accuse Me, Flashing,
Hang On Sloopy, Twist And Shout, Bo Diddley, Tutti Frutti, Lucille.
Personnel
Jimi Hendrix (guitar, vocals); with either Curtis Knight or Little
Richard.
Producer
Ed Chalpin (Curtis Knight tracks); remainder unidentified.
Original Release Date
September, 1974
Label & Catalogue No.
Ember EMB 3428. Subsequently re-issued by Bulldog Records as BDL
2010, retitled TWENTY GOLDEN PIECES OF JIMI HENDRIX, in 1979.

MIDNIGHT LIGHTNING

Tracks
Beginnings, Blue Suede Shoes, Gypsy Boy, Hear My Train, Machine Gun, Midnight Lightning, Once I Had A Woman, Trashman.
Personnel
Jimi Hendrix (guitar, vocals), Jeff Mironov (guitar), Bob Babbit (bass), Alan Schwartzenberg (drums), Lance Quinn (guitar), Jimmy Maeulen (percussion), Mitch Mitchell (drums), Buddy Lucas (harmonica).
Producers
Alan Douglas, Tony Bongiovi
Original Release Date
December, 1975
Label & Catalogue No.
Polydor 2310 415. USA: Warner Reprise 2229.

CRASH LANDING

Tracks
Message To Love, Somewhere Over The Rainbow, Crash Landing, Come Down Hard On Me, Peace In Mississippi, With The Power, Stone Free Again, Captain Coconut.
Personnel
Jimi Hendrix (guitar, vocals), Billy Cox (bass), Jimmy Maeulen (drums), Buddy Miles (drums), Jeff Mironov (guitar), Alan Schwartzberg (drums).
Producers
Alan Douglas, Tony Bongiovi
Original Release Date
September, 1975
Label & Catalogue No.
Polydor 2310 398. USA: Warner Reprise 2204.

JIMI HENDRIX

Tracks
All Along The Watchtower, Angel, The Drifter's Escape, Ezy Rider, House Burning Down, Izabella, Johnny B. Goode, Little Miss Lover, Little Wing, Love Or Confusion, Power To Love, Voodoo Chile.
Personnel
Jimi Hendrix (guitar, vocals) plus various (compilation album).
Producers
Jimi Hendrix, Chas Chandler (certain tracks only).
Original Release Date
March, 1975
Label & Catalogue No.
Polydor 2343 080 (currently cassette only 3192 205)

Title

JIMI HENDRIX VOL. 2

Tracks

Are You Experienced, Bold As Love, Can You See Me, Castles Made Of Sand, Crosstown Traffic, Freedom, Gypsy Eyes, I Don't Live Today, In From The Storm, Long Hot Summer Night, Red House, Remember, Spanish Castle Magic, Stone Free, Straight Ahead.

Personnel

Jimi Hendrix (guitars, vocals) plus various (compilation album).

Producers

Jimi Hendrix, Chas Chandler (certain tracks only).

Original Release Date

October, 1976

Label & Catalogue No.

Polydor 2343 086 (currently casette only Polydor 3192 313).

Title

FOR REAL

Tracks

Red House, Peoples Peoples, Blue Blues, Go Go Shoes, Good Time Bring My Baby Back, Suspicious, Hot Trigger, Voice In The Wind, Goodbye Bessie Mae, Sweet Thang, Groovemaker, Wipe The Sweat, Under The Table (Part 1), Psycho, Good Feeling, Fox, More Sweat, Under The Table (Part 2).

Personnel

Jimi Hendrix (guitar, vocals); see note below.

Producers

John Brantley, Lee Moses; certain tracks unidentified

Original Release Date

November, 1976

Label & Catalogue No.

DJM DJLMD 8011 (now deleted); subsequently re-issued by Audio Fidelity AFESD 1037 (February, 1982).

Note: For details on personnel, see "The Genius of Hendrix" elsewhere in this listing.

Title

FRIENDS FROM THE BEGINNING (with Little Richard)

Tracks

Whole Lotta Shaking, Goodnight Irene, Going A Knocking, Going Home Tomorrow, Belle Stars, Tutti Frutti, Lawdy Miss Clawdie, Why Don't You Love Me, Lucille, Hound Dog, Money Honey, Funny Fish Rag.

Personnel

Little Richard (keyboards, vocals), Jimi Hendrix (guitar), plus others.

Original Release Date

1977

Label & Catalogue No.

Ember EMB 3434

Title

THE ESSENTIAL JIMI HENDRIX

Tracks
All Along The Watchtower, Are You Experienced, Bold As Love, The Burning Of The Midnight Lamp, Castles Made Of Sand, Dolly Dagger, Drifting, Ezy Rider, Freedom, Gypsy Eyes, Have You Ever Been To Electric Ladyland, House Burning Down, If Six Was Nine, Izabella, Little Miss Lover, Little Wing, Purple Haze, Room Full Of Mirrors, Stepping Stone, Still Raining Still Dreaming, Third Stone From the Sun, Voodoo Chile.

Personnel
Jimi Hendrix (guitar, vocals) plus various (compilation album)

Producers
Jimi Hendrix, Chas Chandler (certain tracks only).

Original Release Date
1978

Label & Catalogue No.
Polydor 2612 034. USA: Warner Reprise 2RS 2245

Title

NINE TO THE UNIVERSE

Tracks
Nine To The Universe, Jimi/Jimmy/Jam, Young/Hendrix, Easy Blues, Drone Blues.

Personnel
Jimi Hendrix (guitar, vocals), Billy Cox (bass), Buddy Miles (drums), Jim McCarty (guitar), Roland Robinson (bass), Larry Young (organ), Larry Lee (guitar).

Producer
Alan Douglas

Original Release Date
June, 1980

Label & Catalogue No.
Polydor POLS 1023

Title

STONE FREE

Tracks
All Along The Watchtower, Angel, Are You Experienced, Castles Made Of Sand, Crosstown Traffic, The Drifter's Escape, Ezy Rider, Johnny B. Goode, Little Wing, Long Hot Summer Night, Red House, Stone Free.

Personnel
Jimi Hendrix (guitar, vocals) plus various (compilation album).

Producer
Jimi Hendrix, Chas Chandler (certain tracks only).

Original Release Date
June 1980

Label & Catalogue No.
Polydor 2343 114

Title

WOKE UP THIS MORNING AND FOUND MYSELF DEAD

Tracks
Red House, Woke Up This Morning And You Find Yourself Dead, Bleeding Heart, Morrison's Lament, Tomorrow Never Knows, Uranus Rock, Outside Woman Blues, Sunshine Of Your Love.
Personnel
Jimi Hendrix (guitar, vocals), Johnny Winter (guitar), Randy Hobbs (bass), Randy Z (drums), Jim Morrison (harmonica, vocals, abuse, obscenities, mumbling*), Buddy Miles (drums).
Producer
Unidentified; Michael Jeffery (executive).
Original Release Date
September, 1980
Label & Catalogue No.
Red Lightnin' RL 0015
*As stated in liner notes!

Title

THE ESSENTIAL JIMI HENDRIX VOL. 2

Tracks
Crosstown Traffic, Fire, Foxy Lady, Hey Joe, I Don't Live Today, Machine Gun, The Star Spangled Banner, Wild Thing, The Wind Cries Mary.
Personnel
Jimi Hendrix (guitar, vocals) plus various (compilation album).
Producers
Jimi Hendrix, Chas Chandler (certain tracks only).
Original Release Date
January, 1981
Label & Catalogue No.
Polydor 2311 014

Title

COSMIC TURNAROUND

Tracks
No Such Animal Part 1, Tomorrow, No Such Animal Part 2, Come On Baby 1, Come On Baby II, I Love My Baby, Down Now, Louisville.
Personnel
Jimi Hendrix (guitar, vocals), rest unknown.
Producer

Original Release Date
June, 1981
Label & Catalogue No.
Audo Fidelity AFELP 1002

Title

THE GENIUS OF HENDRIX (4 Record set)

Tracks
Red House, Sweet Thing, Blues Blues, Groovemaker, Peoples Peoples,
She's A Fox, Whoa Eeh, Gonna Take A Lot, Lime Lime, Wipe The
Sweat, Wipe The Sweat (sequel 1), Wipe The Sweat (sequel 2),
Goodbye Bessie May, Two In One Goes, A Mumblin' Word, Miracle
Worker, From This Day On, Human Heart, Feel The Soul, All Alone,
Get Down, So Called Friend, Girl So Fine, Every Little Bit Hurts,
You Say You Love Me, Good Feeling, Voice In The Wind, Suspicious,
Hot Trigger, Good Times, Bring My Baby Back, Go Go Shoes (pt 1),
Go Go Shoes (pt 2).
Personnel
Jimi Hendrix (guitar, vocals); see note below.
Producers
John Brantley, Lee Moses; certain tracks unidentified.
Original Release Date
November, 1981
Label & Catalogue No.
Audio Fidelity AFEH 1027
Note: The personnel on the first three tracks is believed to include
Johnny Winter (guitar, vocals), Jim Morrison (vocals, percussion),
Noel Redding (bass), Mitch Mitchell (drums). These tracks emanate
from a jam session at the Record Plant Studios, New York, sometime
during early 1970. On the remaining tracks the personnel includes
Lonnie Youngblood (reeds, vocals), Herman Hitson (guitar), Lee
Moses (guitar) and various unidentified players.

Half the tracks on this album were at one time available on "For
Real" (DJM DJLMD 8011), now deleted; same tracks currently
available on "For Real' (Audio Fidelity AFESD 1037) — see listing
elsewhere.

Title

HIGH LIVE AND DIRTY

Tracks
F.H.I.T.A., No! No!, In The Morning, Jimi's Blues, Peoples Peoples.
Personnel
Jimi Hendrix (guitar, vocals), rest unknown.
Producer

Original Release Date
March, 1982
Label & Catalogue No.
Audio Fidelity AFEMP 1031

Title

VOODOO CHILE

Tracks
Voodoo Chile (Slight Return), Power To Love, Freedom, Spanish
Castle Magic, Gypsy Eyes, Love Or Confusion, 51st Anniversary,
Little Miss Love, I'm Your Hoochie Coochie Man, Izabella, House
Burning Down, Bold As Love.
Personnel
Jimi Hendrix (guitar, vocals) plus various (compilation album).
Producers
Jimi Hendrix, Chas Chandler (certain tracks only).
Original Release Date
June, 1982
Label & Catalogue No.
Polydor 2343 115

Title

THE JIMI HENDRIX CONCERTS

Fire, I Don't Live Today, Red House, Stone Free, Are You Experienced,
Little Wing, Voodoo Chile, Bleeding Heart, Hey Joe, Wild Thing,
Hear My Train A'Coming.
Personnel
Jimi Hendrix (guitar, vocals), Noel Redding (bass), Mitch Mitchell
(drums), Billy Cox (bass on Red House and Hey Joe).
Producer
Alan Douglas
Original Release Date
August, 1982
Label & Catalogue No.
CBS 88592
Note: Live performances recorded at various locations in the UK and
US between 1968 and 1970.

Title

KALEIDOSCOPE

Tracks
Everything, You Got It, Nobody Can Change Me, Everything You Get,
Night Life, Edda Mae, Find Someone, By My Baby.
Personnel
Jimi Hendrix (guitar, vocals), rest unknown.
Producer
Unidentified
Original Release Date
September, 1982
Label & Catalogue No.
Audio Fidelity AFELP 1040

Title

MOODS

Tracks
A Mumblin' Word, Miracle Worker, From This Day On, Human Heart, Feel That Soul, All Alone, Get Down, So Called Friend, Girl So Fine, Every Little Bit Hurts, You Say You Love Me.
Personnel
Jimi Hendrix (guitar, vocals); remainder unidentified (see note).
Producer
John Brantley
Original Release Date
November, 1982
Label & Catalogue No.
Phoenix PHX 1020
Note: These tracks, previously released by Audio Fidelity (see elsewhere), now made available as budget re-issue.
   Additional personnel believed to be Lonnie Youngblood (reeds, vocals), Herman Hitson (guitar), Lee Moses (guitar) and others unidentified.

Title

ROOTS OF HENDRIX

Tracks
Wipe The Sweat, Wipe The Sweat (segue 1), Wipe The Sweat (segue 2), Goodby Bessie Mae, Two In One Goes, All I Want, Under The Table (Part 1), Under The Table (Part 2), Psycho.
Personnel
Jimi Hendrix (guitar, vocals); remainder unidentified (see note).
Producer
John Brantley
Original Release Date
November, 1982
Label & Catalogue No.
Phoenix PHX 1026
Note: These tracks, previously released by Audio Fidelity (see elsewhere), now made available as budget re-issue.
   Additional personnel believed to be Lonnie Youngblood (reeds, vocals), Herman Hitson (guitar), Lee Moses (guitar) and others unidentified.

Title

FREE SPIRIT

Tracks
Hey Leroy, Free Spirit, House Of The Rising Sun, Something You Got,
Let The God Sing, She's A Fox.
Personnel
Jimi Hendrix (guitar, vocals); remainder unidentified.
Producer
Unidentified
Original Release Date
November, 1982
Label & Catalogue No.
Phoenix PHX 1012

Title

HENDRIX IN MEMORIUM

Tracks
Ballad of Jimi, No Business, Future Trip (Day Tripper Part 2), Gotta
Have A New Dress, Hornet's Nest, Don't Accuse Me, Flashing,
Hush Now, Knock Yourself Out, Happy Birthday, Get That Feeling,
Strange Things, Odd Ball, Love Love, Simon Says, Gloomy Monday,
Welcome Home.
Personnel
Jimi Hendrix (guitar, vocals), Curtis Knight.
Producer
Ed Chalpin
Original Release Date
Unknown
Label & Catalogue No.
London 2LP 3001/2

Title

JIMI HENDRIX & THE ISLEY BROTHERS

Tracks
Move Over, Let Me Dance, Testify, Wild Little Tiger, Simon Says,
Looking For A Love, The Last Girl, Have You Ever Been Disappointed.
Personnel
The Isley Brothers, Jimi Hendrix (guitar).
Producer

Original Release Date
Unknown
Label & Catalogue No.
Buddah TNS 3007 (USA)
Note: These tracks, recorded in New York in 1964, have never been
officially released in the UK. In actuality Hendrix was playing as a
session musician and, when originally released in the US, he received
no credit. Only later, when Hendrix became popular, were the tracks
re-issued by Buddah.

PROTEUS ROCKS

The Best Rock 'n' Roll Reading from Proteus

☐ **TOYAH**
An illustrated fan's eyeview much-liked by Toyah herself.
by Gaynor Evans
UK £1.95
US $3.95

☐ **REGGAE: DEEP ROOTS MUSIC**
The definitive history of reggae. A major TV tie-in.
by Howard Johnson and Jim Pines
UK £5.95
US $10.95

☐ **BOOKENDS**
The first full study of Simon and Garfunkel, their joint and solo careers.
by Patrick Humphries
UK £5.95
US $10.95

☐ **PRETENDERS**
The first full study of this powerful and turbulent band.
by Chris Salewicz
UK £3.95
US $7.95

☐ **LOU REED**
A definitive profile of this almost reclusive figure.
by Diana Clapton
UK £4.95
US $9.95.

☐ **JAMES LAST**
A fully illustrated study of this world phenomenon of popular music.
by Howard Elson
UK £4.95
US $9.95

☐ **RARE RECORDS**
A complete illustrated guide to wax trash and vinyl treasures.
by Tom Hibbert
UK £4.95
US $9.95

☐ **THE PERFECT COLLECTION**
The 200 greatest albums, the 100 greatest singles selected and discussed by leading rock journalists.
Edited by Tom Hibbert
UK £4.95
US $9.95

☐ **EARLY ROCKERS**
All the seminal figures of rock 'n' roll:
Berry, Little Richard, Jerry Lee, Presley et al.
by Howard Elson
UK £4.95
US $9.95

KATE BUSH ☐
Complete illustrated story of this unique artist.
by Paul Kerton
UK £3.95
US $7.95

BLACK SABBATH ☐
Heavy Metal Superstars.
by Chris Welch
UK £4.95
US $9.95

A-Z OF ROCK GUITARISTS ☐
First illustrated encyclopaedia of guitar greats.
by Chris Charlesworth
UK £5.95
US $10.95

A-Z OF ROCK DRUMMERS ☐
Over 300 great drummers in this companion to ROCK GUITARISTS.
by Harry Shapiro
UK £5.95
US $10.95

CHUCK BERRY ☐
The definitive biography of the original Mr Rock 'n' Roll.
by Krista Reese
UK £4.95
US $8.95

A CASE OF MADNESS ☐
A big illustrated guide for fans of this insane band.
by Mark Williams
UK only £1.95

TALKING HEADS ☐
The only illustrated book about one of the most innovative bands of the 70s and 80s.
by Krista Reese
UK £4.95
US $9.95

DURAN DURAN ☐
The best-selling illustrated biography.
UK £1.95
US $3.95

A TOURIST'S GUIDE TO JAPAN ☐
Beautifully illustrated study of Sylvian and his colleagues.
by Arthur A. Pitt.
UK £1.95
US $3.95

ILLUSTRATED POP QUIZ ☐
Over 400 impossible questions for pop geniuses only.
by Dafydd Rees and Barry Lazell
UK £2.95
US $5.95

order form overleaf